When We Can't Talk Anymore

Stories about couples who learned how
to communicate again.

STEVE WILKE
DAVE & NETA JACKSON

LIVING BOOKS®
Tyndale House Publishers, Inc.
Wheaton, Illinois

Library of Congress Catalog Card Number 91-67650
ISBN 0-8423-7987-8

99 98 97 96 95 94 93
9   8   7   6   5   4   3

C O N T E N T S

Introduction

This year Dave and I (Neta Jackson) will be celebrating our silver wedding anniversary. We'll probably throw a party and invite all our friends and relations then sneak away for a weekend alone to reflect on twenty-five years of married life.

What a long way we've come! But it hasn't all been easy, and one of our biggest hurdles—especially in the early years—was the problem of *uncommunicated expectations*.

Idealism was the first stumbling block. As a young bride I thought a caring and sensitive husband would anticipate my needs and desires and take the initiative to meet them without me having to say a thing. So we ended up having typical interactions like this:

Me (coming home from work at the end of the day): "Boy, am I tired." (That's what I said. What I meant was, "I sure would like help making supper.")

Him: "Yeah, I had a rough day too. Why don't we just relax tonight in front of the TV?"

Me (suddenly irritated because he

didn't "catch the hook"): "Can't. I have to wash the floor tonight."

Him (incredulous): "Tonight? You just said you were tired! It looks fine to me. Let's relax tonight—there's a good movie on at eight."

Me: "Forget it! I've got to start supper." Which I did, feeling not only tired but unappreciated, overworked, and saddled with an insensitive husband. I also washed the floor that night, sighing now and then. He ignored me. That made me mad.

Sometimes my inner expectations took the form of little tests. *I wish,* I'd think to myself, *that Dave would offer to give me a backrub from time to time, not because I ask, but just because he knows I enjoy them and he wants to do something nice for me.* But if too many days went by without that offer, I'd start feeling unloved.

Unfortunately, a pattern of poor communication was being set up, and it got worse. Dave's enjoyment of TV clashed with my image and expectations of what he *should* like to do. And with the "consciousness-raising" of the women's movement, I began to have some new expectations of him—largely uncommunicated. When I did discuss them, my words or tone of voice conveyed disapproval, frustration, or blame. Dave would end up feeling attacked or blamed and would usually back off, leaving us both defensive and too often . . . silent.

We were in danger of drifting into a situation where we couldn't talk anymore. Fortunately, over the years we've learned some principles that have helped us.

• *Make your needs or wishes known,* instead of expecting your spouse to know automatically what they are. (I was surprised at how much pride is involved in this!)

• *Don't "test" the other's love.* This is game playing at its worst and is totally unfair to the other person. When I'm tempted to feel sorry for myself, I ask, "Am I looking for ways to show my husband that *he* is loved?"

• *State your needs simply; don't generalize or add blame* to the situation. ("Could you help peel these carrots? I'm running behind schedule"—not, "Why don't you ever help with supper?")

• *Agree ahead of time on mutual expectations.* Thinking ahead to problematic or recurring situations helps. (Does "leaving early" on the family vacation mean 5:30 A.M. or 8:00 A.M.? Who puts which kids to bed which nights? "Why don't I make breakfast while you make school lunches?")

• *Don't have "expectations" for things not agreed on ahead of time.* "Requests" should accept no as a possible answer.

• *Be specific* if something is bothering you. Don't make vague comments that give hidden messages ("I wish people would pick up after themselves around here!"), leaving others feeling uncomfortable and defensive.

• *Timing is important.* Right in the middle of an upsetting situation is not the time to unload general feelings. Deal with the immediate situation in a simple way; later talk about expectations for the future.

• *Be willing to disagree, compromise, or take turns* when personal tastes differ. (We sometimes like to do different things with our leisure time—so we take turns making plans for our night out.

The important thing is that we like being together!)

• *Remember that love is forgiveness.* This is probably the most important principle we've learned. Knowing that neither one of us hurts the other intentionally helps take away the hurt and the urge to blame when we fail to live up to the other's expectations. Rather than expecting perfection, we are not surprised by our human weaknesses and mistakes. Just as we live daily in God's forgiveness, our own love must be a forgiving love.[*]

As you read the true stories in this book, you'll see how these and other principles were played out in the lives of other couples. Some had despaired— even to the point of divorce—of ever being able to talk constructively and lovingly again. But they found hope and learned new ways to communicate.

Each couple has participated in Recovery of Hope, a program sponsored by a network of counseling centers around

---

[*]Neta Jackson, adapted from "The Stumbling Block of Uncommunicated Expectations," in *Husbands & Wives*, ed. Howard Hendricks et al. (Wheaton, Ill.: Victor Books, 1988), pp. 302-304.

the country. Every day marital conflicts are resolved, hurts are healed, brokenness made whole—but most people do not hear about these successes. And because they do not hear, they have no hope when their own marriage gets in trouble. The Recovery of Hope Network has helped hundreds of couples restore hope in their marriage primarily by giving them an opportunity to hear other couples who have been through the worst tell their stories of reconciliation. The message is clear: with help, marriages can be restored. You can learn to communicate and love one another again!

Throughout the book and especially in the fourth chapter, Dr. Steve Wilke provides insights into why and how communication breaks down in marriages and how it can be rebuilt. Dr. Wilke is a licensed clinical psychologist and founding president of Recovery of Hope Network, Inc. He now works as a consultant to the Network.

Dave and Neta Jackson
Evanston, Illinois

CHAPTER ONE

"What's the Matter? Have a Bad Day?"

Bob Garrett had put in a hard day. It had been a good day, but since he was out west of town, he thought he ought to stop in and see old man Kramer. It wouldn't take long, and with it almost dry enough to get into the fields, Kramer might be ready to spring for a new plow. Everyone knew he'd needed one for two years now. But old Kramer was one to get every ounce of work out of a piece of machinery before he'd get a new one.

Bob glanced at his watch—5:37. If he headed for home, he could get there by dinnertime. He braked at the stop sign at County 38. Left for home, or right for Kramer's? Which would it be?

He swung the wheel hard to the right and stepped on the gas. "No sense driving all the way out here again," he muttered to himself. Besides, if he didn't get to Kramer soon, the old skinflint would get out his welder and convince himself that his repairs would make do for another season.

When Bob finally got home, it was nearly eight-thirty, but he'd made another sale and a handsome commission too. So what if he had missed dinner? He didn't mind the sacrifice. He knew how to be the number-one salesman. It was all in the timing.

"Hey, Rhonda, guess what!" he called as he swung open the door and hung his coat on the hook.

"Daddy," yelled five-year-old Jackie as he ran to hug Bob's legs. Esther came toddling after. Nicholas, seven, said, "Hi, Dad," without looking up from the TV.

Bob whipped off his DeKalb Corn hat and put it sideways on Jackie's head. "How's my boy? Did you feed your rabbits today?" Bob reached down and swooped up Esther and gave her a kiss as he hobbled on into the living room with Jackie hanging on like a lead boot. Bob could hear Anna squalling from the bedroom. He made his way down the toy-cluttered hall. Rhonda was changing the baby.

"Hi, Dear. Guess what!"

Rhonda didn't answer. She didn't even look up to acknowledge him. *He doesn't care about anything but himself,* she thought. *And I'm not going to give him the satisfaction of fawning all over him again.*

"What's the matter?" asked Bob. "Have a bad day?"

"Your food's in the oven." Rhonda decided that if Bob couldn't tell by looking at her that the kids had been driving her crazy, and that she didn't feel good, and that she wished he had come home sooner, then it was his problem! She was too angry to be in any mood to explain.

Finally free of his "lead boot," Bob put Esther down and went into the kitchen. He opened the oven. There was his plate, all right, piled high and still warm—Jell-O salad included.

Bob sat at the kitchen table picking at

his food. He could never understand
Rhonda's moods. The best he had been
able to do was lie low until she snapped
out of them, but man, could she make a
guy mad! She was lucky he put up with
her. After all, he'd worked his tail off all
day, and he was making pretty good
money too. What'd she have to be upset
about?

He left the mashed potatoes, red with
Jell-O juice, on his plate and went to his
desk in the den. There in the quiet with
the door shut, he filled out his reports
and planned the next day.

It was nearly ten o'clock when he
came out. The kids were gone all except
Nicholas who was still watching TV.
"Hey, Buddy, don't you think it's time for
bed?" he said.

"How come? Mom didn't say so."

"Mom's not talkin' to you. I am."

"Yeah, but she doesn't make me go to
bed this early."

"'Yeah, but' nothin'. Who do you
think's in charge around here, anyway?"

"But I always watch "Star Trek."
Come on, Dad. It's almost over."

Bob looked at his watch. What could

he say? He sat down in his chair and watched the Enterprise streak through outer space while his mind streaked through inner space. He was losing it. Whatever he had had in this family was slipping through his grasp, and he had no idea why.

When Rhonda finished putting the little ones to bed she gathered up another load of laundry and headed for the basement. She hated that basement. It was always so dark and damp, and one of these days she was going to trip on the stairs and break her neck. She didn't know why Bob had insisted on putting the washer and dryer down there. So what if the previous owner had done it? There was plenty of room on the back porch. Maybe she'd ask one more time.

When she came up, she walked down the hall and looked into the front room as she leaned against the doorway. Bob didn't look up from the TV, even though Rhonda was positive he knew she was standing there. To get him to do anything around the house was like . . . well, it was as hard as it had been to get her dad to do anything. The only thing to be said for

Bob was that he wasn't an alcoholic like her dad had been. But what difference did it make? Bob was just as hard to live with. Rhonda went on into the kitchen and began to do the dishes.

When Bob asked Rhonda if she had had a bad day, she wouldn't tell him. Sometimes communication deteriorates so badly that seemingly correct words won't work. Rhonda didn't believe Bob really wanted to know how she was. She probably took his question more as a challenge: "Why are you in this mood?" But by not talking, she guaranteed inadequate communication. Similarly, Bob's conclusion that all he could do was wait out Rhonda's "mood" assured that he wouldn't understand any more about the problem.

Vows to one's self, such as "I'm not gonna talk" or "I'll just lie low until she snaps out of it," guarantee that things won't improve. But Rhonda and Bob's communication problems had begun much earlier.

Rhonda had been raised mostly by her mom. Because of her father's alcoholism, he just never seemed to be home.

When he was home, there were a lot of arguments and even occasional physical fights. Rhonda hated what drinking did to her father and vowed that she would never marry a man like him.

She had met Bob at a church youth group and was immediately attracted to his beautiful green eyes and warm smile. They went together only a short time before Rhonda decided that she had finally found someone who would love her and cherish her forever— "someone who would treat me like I'm a precious piece of gold" is the way she remembers him.

But during their four years of dating, they too argued a lot and even fought physically. When Bob mistreated her, Rhonda would tell him she was going to find someone else. He would slap her and twist her arm until she would promise not to leave him. She just thought it was his way of showing her that he cared for her. And she wanted so much for Bob to love her and make her feel loved.

Bob had been raised in a Christian home. His mother was a homemaker;

his father a farmer who worked such long and hard hours that Bob remembers having only a few good times with him. His mother did most of the care for the children and most of the household chores too. Bob recalls that she "tried to teach me that it was OK for a man to do some things around the house, but I saw very little being done by my father, so I never figured it was necessary for me to do things like cleaning my room or making my bed." Very early, his family labeled him "the ornery one," and so he *felt* "ornery," as though he didn't quite measure up. He remembers often wondering if he had been adopted.

During his teenage years Bob's relationship with his father deteriorated even further. They seemed to disagree on everything. Now Bob realizes that all he really wanted from his father was some type of affirmation. "Maybe I started becoming like him just to win his approval. I am sure he assumed I knew he loved me as his son, but I wanted so badly for him to take me aside and talk to me alone about our problems and to tell me that he loved me." But Bob's father was too busy farming, going to church, and trying to create the "good Christian family."

Even when Bob got married, he was still trying to win his father's approval by doing things the way his dad had done: work long hours, make lots of money, take the family to church, and leave the housework to the wife.

Rhonda's reasons for marrying Bob were partly because she loved him but also partly to get away from her own home situation. She knew their courtship had some rough edges, but she thought they would both be more grown-up after marriage, and she expected Bob to be everything her father wasn't. What a disappointment! Even though they both worked, Bob never helped her with any of the housework.

When Rhonda did ask for help, Bob would say, "What for? That's your job." Rhonda never let him know how much that kind of comment hurt. She just kept it inside and stewed about it. Slowly she began to feel trapped. Every time she looked at Bob, she kept seeing her father.

Three years into the marriage they had a baby boy. Again, Rhonda expected help with diaper changes, feedings, and getting up in the night. But Bob said there was no way he was changing diapers, and when the baby cried he'd say, "Shut that kid up!" Eventually there were four children, and the situation hadn't changed a bit.

Bob's job of selling farm equipment kept him on the road for many long hours. He would be up early and home late and didn't really seem to see Rhonda or the kids either coming or going. Rhonda, on the other hand, had the children by herself all day and all night—except Sunday. They seldom went anywhere together except to church. And on Sundays, when they came home, Rhonda felt the only thing Bob did was sleep or sit in front of the TV with a ball game on. She felt lonely for his company. She wanted him to hold her and ask how her day or week had been, but he was often so exhausted from work that he didn't want to talk. "And the only touching or holding I got was when we had sex," Rhonda recalls.

"Even that became degrading to me because I felt used; I was just there to satisfy him."

It's always a mistake to depend on your partner magically changing after marriage. Everybody changes. But basing a marriage on the hope that helpful change will just happen is a dangerous hope. Bob and Rhonda both put their relationship under a strain of uncommunicated expectations from the start. Both longed for these needs to be met automatically without needing to listen closely to or share openly with each other.

Many people marry believing that intolerable conditions will improve. Those conditions do improve if there is a sufficiently strong commitment to the marriage. However, things often get worse before they get better. This time of getting worse happens because we are so reluctant to make waves—disclose our feelings, confront ourselves, and face our situation. The hope that the problems will just effortlessly go away is an enticing fantasy that is hard to let go.

One morning as Bob was about ready to go off to work, Rhonda handed him a note:

> I'm tired: tired of hearing your excuses for not doing things around the house, tired of you being late, tired of you making us late because of your long hours. I'm tired of having to do all the child care and housework. We really need to take time to talk and work out some things!

"What's this?" Bob asked.

"A note. Just read it!"

"I did. But why a note? Can't you just talk to me?"

"No, but we need to talk."

"Well, then, just do it. You've got a mouth. This is silly!" He tossed the crumpled note in the trash as he went out the door.

Bob never mentioned the note when he came home that night nor in the days that followed. From his perspective, what was there to say? He assumed that if Rhonda really wanted to talk, she could come to him in person. But from Rhonda's perspective, every time she had tried to talk to Bob, she had gone away feeling like everything was her fault.

So Rhonda withdrew more and more and kept her wants, needs, hurts, anger, and fear inside. If Bob didn't want to hear about her, she decided she wasn't going to push herself onto him. But she couldn't seem to let anyone else know how lonely and hurt she was either . . . not even their pastor. At church she didn't have any close friends, and she slowly came to the conclusion that her hopes for a good marriage had all been a mirage. Maybe no one had it any better than her mother and father's marriage. Maybe that was what life was like. After all, that was all she'd ever seen. So she put on a big smile at church, or when others were around, so no one would know how lost she felt inside.

No one, that is, until she met a very understanding friend one day when she was visiting her parents. He was a neighbor who came over just to be friendly. Rhonda went back again and again, and he would always just "happen" to come over. As the relationship grew, Rhonda became very close friends with him. She enjoyed his company because it felt so good just to be noticed and to be able to share problems with him as a human being. She felt he was there when she needed him.

But as such things tend to do, it became a lot more than just friendship. They started to have an affair, and Rhonda knew right away that what she wanted was out of her marriage. She recalls: "I just had to have this man because I could be me when I was around him. He seemed to love me no matter what I looked like or felt like. He was a loving, caring, compassionate, considerate person who seemed to love me for me—everything that Bob didn't do."

One day Bob got a call from Rhonda at work: "You've gotta come home right now."

"What?" Bob said.

"Just come home—now."

"But it's the middle of the day."

"I know, but it's urgent."

"Is it the kids? Has something happened to one of them?"

"No. It's me. We need to talk about me."

"Why, for heaven's sake? Why right now? Can't this wait?"

"Just come home." And then she hung up.

Bob thought about the call for a moment. He was sure she wasn't hurt, yet there had been a strange determination in her voice. What could it be? He left the office and headed down the highway. *Maybe her parents are ill*, he mused. *No. That couldn't be it. She would have told me on the phone. It's got to be something else—something about us.*

It came to Bob that for several weeks Rhonda had had no emotions, no energy; she could barely care for herself, let alone the children. Why hadn't she talked to him sooner? Whatever it was, it made him angry that she hadn't told him when it was more convenient. This wasn't fair to make a federal case out of whatever it was she wanted to say.

As he drove, a plan grew in his mind: he would drive up shouting, "Where's the fire? Where's the fire?" Or maybe he'd march into the house demanding to confront "the other man" who wanted to take away his wife to live happily ever after somewhere else. He'd do something dramatic to show her how ridiculous it was to call him away from work for something she should have told him at a more appropriate time.

But when he got there and saw the look in her eyes, Bob thought better of himself and listened. And what he heard shook him up. *Why didn't I see it coming?* he wondered later. *I feel so stupid, so blind . . . as if the whole time I've been driving a car down the road with the hood up, not really able to see where I'm going, not really caring, assuming that as long as I do the right things, I'll get there in good shape.*

And then Rhonda said the dreaded words: "The marriage is over, Bob. I'm moving out."

Bob felt like a little boy who had been abandoned by his parents—nowhere to go, not knowing where he was, not knowing what to do. "Is there someone else?" he asked tentatively, sure that there couldn't be and hoping Rhonda would see that moving out wasn't necessary.

"Actually, there is," admitted Rhonda. "And I want to marry him."

Bob was devastated. *How could things have gone so far?* he thought, his mind in a whirl. He had never thought their problems were so big. It seemed to him that Rhonda had done a good job of hiding her discontent, and he accused her of not telling him before things had gotten so serious.

She reminded him of all the times she *had* said something. And then she handed him a crumpled piece of paper. "You remember this?"

He opened it up. It was that silly little note. He felt his face getting hot. "Where'd you get this? Did you fish it out of the trash and keep it all this time? Aw, come on. You didn't expect me to take it seriously. I mean, it was a joke, wasn't it?"

"It was not a joke, and I wrote it only because I couldn't think of anything else to do."

Indeed, how could things have gone so far? Bob had kept his focus on his issues. He had watched only his indicators. Her messages weren't great by his standards; nothing was in the danger zone. But Bob knew little of Rhonda's criteria for a good marriage. He had not taken Rhonda's attempts at communication to heart. He had ignored her requests, dismissed her note as a joke, and had no intention of taking seriously her call for him to come home from work . . . until she dropped the bomb on him. Shock, then bewilderment. How could she have come to this point? Why hadn't he picked up her signals along the way?

For Bob it was time to seek understanding. The changes he would make gave him new life and gave his marriage one last chance. For Rhonda, the time had come for a radical departure from the status quo.

Rhonda did move out, but it was no solution. She missed the kids and didn't know which way to turn. Before long she came back. Then she left again. She remembers feeling like she was on a rubber band. "Finally," she says, "that rubber band snapped." She decided that she should be home with the children. But once back, she couldn't motivate herself; she couldn't think straight, couldn't do household chores, couldn't get herself dressed. She didn't care if she lived or died. Sometimes she would picture a car running into hers and killing her or injuring her badly, but she didn't have the nerve to take her own life.

"It was almost impossible trying to take care of four kids when I didn't care about anything," Rhonda admits. "It was so frustrating not to be able to make myself get up and do something. I wanted to, but I just couldn't. It was like I had weights or heavy chains on my wrists, feet, and shoulders so I couldn't move."

Rhonda was in this state for quite a while before she finally was able to do a bit of work around the house. "But," she says, "I still had no love or respect for Bob. The hurts, anger, and bitterness were so strong that I found myself hoping that he would die so my problems would be solved. I had waited so long for him to love me that I had given up.

I had no hope that he would ever love me the way I wanted and needed to be loved."

Rhonda remembers hating the way she was and calling out to God several times for help. But she felt her prayers weren't being answered. How could she go on living this miserable, bitter, guilty life? "At that time I didn't want to talk to anybody else," she says. "I didn't know how my church family would react to what I had done. I was afraid and felt totally helpless."

But during this time some good things were happening to Bob. Rhonda may have found someone else (though it hadn't worked out yet for her to marry him), but Bob began to see that he, too, had an "affair" going; his mistress was his job. And it wasn't a recent affair, either. He had put his job first from the beginning of their marriage. Being "top dog" among the salesmen and making more than the year before made him feel good. When his work increased, Bob just worked harder. He had trouble delegating jobs to others. Because he had learned how to do things right and quicker than anyone else, he figured if he let someone else do it, he would just have to do it over again anyway.

"Not only had this approach made me a slave to my work," reflects Bob, "but I now realize that I brought the same attitudes home. Everything had to be done my way, and I gave no consideration to Rhonda's opinions. Even when we would take a rare outing—like going out to eat—we always ended up eating where I wanted to eat. It was my choice that kept the washer and dryer in the basement. And I wouldn't pay any attention when Rhonda ask me to fix little things around the house unless I was the one who decided they needed doing. I was so used to thinking that my ideas and way of doing things were so much better than hers—or anyone else's for that matter—that I just dismissed her requests even when she was telling me we needed to talk."

But after Bob realized what he'd been doing, he was afraid it was too late. Even though Rhonda had moved back home, it felt like an enormous wall divided them. He wanted to have a deeper relationship with her, but he didn't know how to develop one. He wanted her to have friends and relatives over for get-togethers, but she would become upset and wouldn't even consider the idea—mainly because she didn't want other people to discover what was going on in their marriage.

Even when Bob tried to take Rhonda out—just the two of them—she would always use the excuse that she didn't want to leave the kids with someone else. Bob began to feel hopeless. He tried talking about vacation plans or the possibility of moving up to a newer, nicer house, but Rhonda didn't want to think or talk about the future at all. He wondered if she would ever get over her anger at him.

Then one day their pastor told them about a program to help people struggling in their marriages and suggested that they attend. The program involved an intensive week spent working on their marriage with the assistance of counselors. Both Rhonda and Bob knew that something drastic needed to happen if their marriage was to survive, and so they agreed to try.

At the time it didn't seem that the week-long marriage program helped all that much, but they did learn a lot about themselves. Rhonda found it a real relief to know that she wasn't crazy and that many of her problems were related to her childhood experiences. These insights were significant enough to her that she continued with some further counseling even after they returned home.

Slowly Rhonda began to notice some changes in Bob. He was beginning to become more patient, considerate, compassionate—the husband she had longed for him to be. He would buy her flowers and clothes and leave little notes in the fridge, on the countertop, in the cupboard—wherever he thought she might look. It wasn't that the notes and little gifts were so significant in themselves, but they showed Rhonda that he was thinking of her.

At first she felt confused: "This can't be real. This isn't the Bob I know." She didn't dare to allow herself to trust that it would last. She felt afraid to give in to any kind of love for Bob because she had been hurt so badly and didn't want to leave herself open to more pain. Like an out-of-focus lens on some internal camera, she couldn't get a clear picture of what was happening.

And there was still the "other man." She couldn't let go of him. He, at least, seemed to be *in* focus, and she continued to believe that they needed each other and ought to be together. He seemed so trustworthy and loved only her. At least that's what she thought until the day she found out that she had been dumped for someone else . . . by the very man who had said he would love her forever.

It was a terrible blow, one that made her feel like a part of her had died. And yet, there was some relief in knowing that she was no longer being torn in two. No longer were there two men, but just one.

The choice she had to make at that point was whether to love that man or leave him. She knew, of course, that her decision wouldn't affect just her and

Bob; there were also their four children. As she thought of them and the implications of breaking up the family, she found the courage somewhere deep within to try and love their daddy.

Without consciously knowing it, Rhonda did some things that gave the recovery of their marriage a fighting chance. First, she didn't leave permanently. Second, she prayed to God for help. Third, she gave Bob enough of a chance to notice that he was changing. At this point, God answered Rhonda's prayer for help, though possibly not in the way she expected, when the other man was removed from the picture. This happened even before Rhonda faced that having the affair was wrong. Then, to Rhonda's credit, she took a fourth step: she chose not to break up the family but to try to love her children's father. Taking a step of faith is not throwing all caution to the wind. Rather it is simply being open to new possibilities.

Up until this point, things had been pretty rough for Bob too—not knowing if there was any hope of real change within himself and being even less certain if any change could happen in time to keep Rhonda. Night after night, he would come home wondering if it would be the night she had left for good. But as long as she didn't force him to leave, he felt he should stay at least to show her how much he wanted to change. Early on he decided that the least he could do would be to change his ways and help with the children and some of the housework.

As it became evident to him that the problems he was facing were more than he could handle, he turned to anyone and everyone he could think of for support and encouragement. He talked with their pastor, their families, and other friends. One friend spent a lot of time on several occasions praying with and encouraging him. Bob recalls that even that was a real change for him; he'd never asked anyone for help before.

The real boost for him came when Rhonda consented to go with him to the week of intensive counseling for troubled marriages. "I was really helped by the analysis of my family background," says Bob. "I received the counseling I had needed for a long time and could finally see why some things had happened the way they did. From then on, I began to feel hope, even though there were times when I felt like a stranger in my own house."

Bob finally decided to share about the situation with people in their church—they would hear about it anyway. But for Bob it was a form of confession. "I knew I had failed to be the kind of husband Rhonda needed and deserved, and that I also needed to forgive her for ways in which she had hurt me," says Bob. "I felt that if God would only give me another chance, I would do better. And sharing it set up the opportunity for me to be accountable to others about how I needed to change." The pastor made a statement to regular attenders, urging them not to talk about it to others. If the subject were brought up, they might say, "We know they are having problems and our church loves and is praying for them." This also helped their Christian brothers and sisters to care and pray intelligently for them.

The day that Rhonda told Bob that she had been let down by the other man was a real turning point for Bob. Slowly, he began to feel that she was giving him the chance he wanted to show her that he really could be trusted, that he really cared for her and wanted to meet her emotional needs as he hadn't before.

"As I kept on trying to do the right things—for our marriage, not just for me," Bob says, "Rhonda found that I was less apt to behave as she had come to expect in the past. And did that feel good! The good times began to be really great even though the bad times still felt really bad. Trusting became easier. I could now accept the bad times along with the good. The bad wouldn't be forever."

Though Rhonda was giving Bob a chance, there was no way that she could say she loved him yet. But instead of waiting and hoping for the feeling of love to come, Rhonda did a courageous thing: she *chose* to love. That is, she chose to put into practice the things one does when one loves. As she recalls it, "The more I showed love to Bob and acted the way I would if I really *felt* love toward him, the easier it became. And in time the feelings began to follow. At first they were so tentative that I hardly dared to believe them. But I remember the first day I realized that I was eagerly waiting for him to come home from work—not because I was frustrated at him being away but because I just wanted to see him."

Of course this didn't come overnight, but with time and a husband who was becoming more patient and understanding, it did begin to happen. Slowly, Rhonda began to realize that Bob truly had made some significant changes, and that he had done this for her. A respect and appreciation began to grow for him that she had never dreamed was possible. In time she could honestly say, "I love him and he loves me . . . for me."

Rhonda and Bob have since compared their marriage to a house: "We think of our marriage now like a house that we are building and live in together. The counseling we received made us realize that we were both trying to build without a plan, without the tools we needed, and without the skill to use those tools."

For Bob and Rhonda, the primary tools they lacked were communication skills. For instance, when Bob would come home from work and ask Rhonda how her day had gone, it seemed to her that he surely knew just by looking at the anger showing in her face. If he couldn't tell, it was his problem! She was too angry to explain. But silence was the wrong tool, and it tore down their house faster than they could build it up.

These are some of the communication tools Bob and Rhonda learned to use:

- Make no assumptions. *This tool is like a plumbline that never assumes anything is as it looks and always checks it out. Never assume that the other person can tell what you think or feel by looking at you.*
- Use "I feel . . ." statements. *This simple tool is basically an agreement that it is always OK—and very important—to tell the other person how*

you feel. It's always OK to say, "I feel [so and so]," even though it is not OK to say, "You make me feel [so and so]."

- Practice servant leadership. *One of the things that Bob discovered was that the less he tried to control Rhonda, the more she was open to any leading and suggestions he might have. And when he wasn't intent on controlling, he discovered that he often wanted to do things her way, especially if it brought her joy.*

- Go slowly. *One of the ways to avoid getting into a combative stance with each other is to slow down a conversation. Don't be waiting to jump in with a comeback. When a break comes, remain silent for a moment, thinking about what's been said—Do I really understand?—before you make your point.*

- Watch the timing. *There are times when trying to discuss any difference will be rough—when either of you are tired, are intent on doing something else, or just don't have time for a thorough discussion. It's better to wait* to work things out. But don't sweep the differences under the rug. They do need to be dealt with.

- Stick to the issue. *It's tempting when one feels threatened to mention other problems or to overgeneralize: "You always . . ." This never helps.*

- Acknowledge your contribution to the problem. *Very few problems are completely one-sided. If one person can be big enough to own his or her part, it will be a lot easier for the other person to admit some responsibility, and pretty soon you are half-way to a solution.*

- Affirm your spouse. *Conflict is rough, threatening everyone's self-esteem and personal security. If you don't want communication to end, build the other person up with a touch or a word. This will help you both to keep the issue separate from the person.*

- Learn to say, "Please forgive me," and learn to forgive. *Nothing is more important in reconciliation than asking for forgiveness when you have*

been wrong and forgiving the other
when you have been wronged.
* Work toward resolution. Some *things
are very hard to resolve. But it is
sometimes tempting to quit on rela-
tively easy problems before they are
resolved. Unfinished business piles
up. But you'll feel fresh and accom-
plished every time you really agree on
something.*

Rhonda says that she and Bob are now
able to enjoy their four children in a
way they never did before. "We also
enjoy our intimate times together. It
feels good to know that Bob's touching
and holding means that he really loves
me. We've been using our new communication tools to build a new marriage
bed. I don't feel cheap or degraded any
longer but totally loved."

The Garretts admit they still have
their struggles—especially in communication. And they probably always will.
They still seek counseling, but the direction in which they are headed is no
longer in question. With a kind of wonder that comes from going through the

fire and surviving, Bob says, "We are glad to do the hard work it takes to keep our relationship growing and our communication flowing."

CHAPTER TWO

Married Singles

Eight-year-old Juan grabbed Theresa's hand and ran into their bedroom. He slammed the door. Theresa was already crying, but at least in here she wouldn't be in the way if Mommy threw something or if Daddy hit Mommy.

Through the thin walls Juan could hear the same old argument getting louder: "What do you expect me to do in the evenings? I take care of the kids all day; I've had it! I need a break."

"A break! You've been out every night. Stay home like a decent mother. People are talking."

"I have not been out every night. I was home night before last."

"Yeah, but I'm the one that goes to

work every day. I ought to be able to rest in the evenings—not take care of kids."

"So you don't think what I do is work? Well, then, you can do it yourself! Just because all *you* do is sit around and watch TV every night doesn't mean that I watch the soaps all day. It isn't so easy taking care of kids, you know."

"Big deal. It's not like working in the sawmill."

"Then you do it. Because I'm going out with the girls."

"No, you're not!" yelled Luis. "You've been out three nights this week, and I won't allow it."

"You won't what?"

"I won't allow it!"

"So, you won't *allow* it. Who do you think you are? We'll see who allows what. Where's my coat?"

"You take one more step toward that door, and you'll end up on the floor."

From the crashing that Juan next heard, he knew that his mother had taken the next step. Pretty soon he heard the front door open and his father yell, "If you leave this time, don't ever think about coming back!" A few moments later his mother screamed, and Juan ran to the bedroom window to see what had happened. His mother was on the ground, and his father was kicking her as he yelled, "You're no good! You're just a tramp! I'll find someone else who's a lot better than you." His mother got up and ran to the car and drove off, spraying the fence with gravel from the car's spinning wheels.

As his father stumbled back to the house, Juan could see that tears were streaming down his face.

"Where's Mommy? I want my mommy," wailed two-year-old Theresa.

"Shut up and go to bed," snapped Juan as he shut off the light and flopped onto his bed. He buried his head in his pillow to muffle the sobs that wrenched his body.

This wasn't the first time Maria had walked out on Luis. When Theresa was only six months old, Maria had gotten fed up with Luis just parking himself in front of the TV at night or going out drinking with his buddies on the weekend after she'd been stuck at home just caring for the kids all day. They never talked or did anything together any-more. So she started going out with her girlfriends. At first it was just on the weekends, then gradually on week-nights whenever she could. Luis didn't seem to mind at first, but as time went on, he started giving her a hard time about going out so often. But that didn't stop Maria. She just made up reasons why she *had* to go out.

She became a regular at a couple of bars where she felt she could forget her responsibilities and enjoy herself. Then one night she phoned Luis at three in the morning and told him she wasn't coming home. "I'll get in touch with you later about picking up my things and seeing the kids," she said curtly. Luis demanded an explanation, but Maria just hung up.

Luis was shocked! Had things really gotten that bad?

Maria and Luis had started going to-gether when they were only sixteen and seventeen years old. Actually, Luis found Maria so attractive that he stole her away from his best friend. It wasn't long before everyone saw "Maria and Luis" as a couple and assumed they would stay together forever. In a couple of years they had a little boy, but they didn't get married until two and a half years later. During that time, they were a couple of fun-loving kids who enjoyed playing house together. "We both had a job," remembers Luis, "so money wasn't a problem. At the time we lived near a semi-professional baseball park, and we used to enjoy putting the baby in the stroller and going over to watch a game. We'd hang out with our friends and enjoy their affirmation of us as a couple. I knew Maria was beautiful, and it was an ego boost for me to show her off. We were just having a lot of fun."

Being in love with love is not the same as learning to love a real person for who he or she is. And playing house together isn't the same as building a family together. One thing that Maria and Luis lacked was the skill to communicate effectively with each other. And this deficiency began to take its toll.

When their second child came along, there were more pressures. They had moved into a bigger house, but Maria had quit working outside the home, and so money was much tighter. With Maria at home all day, she didn't have as many social outlets and began to look to Luis for more companionship. However, when he came home tired from work, all he wanted to do was flip on the TV. Though they were thrown more closely together, they found less and less common ground in their relationship.

"I was bored staying alone at home with no one to talk to," admits Maria. "But when Luis came home all he would do is talk *at* me, not with me. He'd ask, 'What's for dinner?' or 'Where's the TV guide?' or make some other remark that one might say to a stranger. There were never any intimate conversations. We never planned together, and he never really took any interest in how I was doing. He expected me to pay the bills and take care of the baby and do the laundry, but he didn't pay any attention to *me*."

With Maria at home with the baby and Luis working harder, they weren't going out much, so they weren't getting as many strokes from other people about being a "darling couple." When they couldn't look outward for fulfillment and found little substance when they looked inward to one another, they both began to want to escape. And they did so by drinking more and more. Luis began to live for the weekends to go out drinking with the boys. Maria would have liked to live for the weekends to be with Luis, but that never happened.

Under these circumstances, it was almost inevitable that what little conversation they did have together soon degenerated into arguments. And with both of them drinking, those arguments became more abusive and even violent.

Finally, Maria had had it and decided to split. Luis knew they had been arguing a lot, but he assumed that was normal in a marriage. When Maria didn't come home in a day or two, he got worried and filed a missing person report with the police. He just couldn't believe she had left him. Maybe she'd had an accident or gotten mugged.

Attractions are mysterious forces. The good feelings of "falling in love" are so strong and wonderful that life can easily be simplified to: "When I'm with you, everything's great; your mere presence is all I need." But what you see is not what you get in marriage. What you see is what you want to see and what you choose to see. For Luis and Maria, their early years of marriage reflected the shallow exposure to their own woundedness and a superficial exploration of each other.

"Looking good" as a couple (as Luis and Maria did to their friends) doesn't take much. But looking good doesn't last; long-lasting relationships require deep knowledge and understanding of the other person. God understands the desire to know fully and to be fully known. Until we start that journey, we have neither the understanding nor the empathy for each other that makes a marital union work. No one can look good and be good all the time.

As demands increase and infatuation wears thin, it's time to become honest and open. But this requires well-developed communication skills—something neither Luis nor Maria had learned. Both knew

something was wrong. Both asked them-
selves, Is marriage supposed to be abusive?
Why am I being attacked? How can she act
this way? How can he treat me this way?
Moving from "looking good" to "being
real" takes a lot of open, intentional com-
munication. At this point, Luis and Maria
simply didn't know how.

It was three weeks before Luis saw Maria again. When he did, he pleaded with
her to come back: "Look, I'll forgive
you," he said. "We'll let bygones be bygones." But Maria wouldn't listen. By
then she had decided she wanted out of
the marriage. She was living with a guy
she'd met at one of the bars, and she
thought she cared about him. But . . . it
didn't last. She ended up moving in with
her parents and getting a job.

When Maria arranged to see the kids,
however, she'd see Luis as well. To her
surprise she realized she missed him;
feelings for him that she thought were
dead began to stir. They started seeing
each other and eventually Maria quit
her job and moved back home. But . . .
something had changed.

"I felt Luis treated me scornfully," Maria recalls. "He wasn't able to forgive me or to forget what had happened. Oh, things would seem fine for awhile until Luis would start drinking—usually on weekends—and then all his anger would come out. He would throw things and even hit me. It was worse than it had ever been, but secretly I felt I deserved to be treated that way for what I'd done, so for a long time I took it."

Things continued in this state for about a year—days when things were OK, followed by screaming fights. Those fights at home became so violent that Maria started going out to bars again just to get away. This time, in addition to drinking, she began to use drugs—anything to escape from the unpleasantness at home.

In some ways, Maria's absence didn't bother Luis very much. He also seemed to enjoy himself more when he was away from Maria and with his friends. "A lot of us guys looked at our wife as someone to get away from for awhile," Luis recalls. "We'd get together to play ball or get drunk or watch a ball game over at someone's house. I guess I felt more confident of myself when I was alone or with the guys. No pressure from the wife, and only me to worry about."

But going their separate ways began to take its toll on the marriage. Luis and Maria had less and less in common. Their friends were different, and all their time was spent apart—Luis at work and Maria with the kids during the day, then each doing their own thing at night or on weekends. She didn't want to hear about his work problems, and he didn't want to hear her complain about her problems with the kids. Furthermore, their approaches to disciplining the children were proving to be more and more in conflict. Maria had grown up in a very strict home and wanted to make sure that their children obeyed. Luis, on the other hand, had "run the streets" when he was a kid. He felt he had turned out OK, so "Why be getting on the kids all the time?"

Soon it seemed that either they had nothing in common or what little they

had to talk about led inevitably to a fight
. . . so they didn't talk. But there was no
stability in a truce. Maria had never
asked for forgiveness for her affair or for
leaving Luis the first time, so she had a
lot of guilt. And Luis still seethed with
resentment. These feelings couldn't be
kept down.

*Oh, for the good old days, when all our
faults were hidden! Terrified of reality, the
natural response is to try to recapture the
past. Let this go; ignore that; put on a
happy face; let's look good again. Like
Adam and Eve in the Garden, we would
like to hide from God and return to a state
of ignorant bliss. But there is no going
back. The realities that we can hurt each
other with disloyalty, jealousy, selfishness,
and rage are now known and documented.
An attempt to pretend to be the "perfect
couple" just won't cut it anymore.*

Before long Luis began to suspect that
Maria was having another affair. He
kept getting reports from friends and
family that they had seen her at this bar
or that club. Sometimes a buddy would

say, "Say, Luis, saw your wife last night over at the Black Raven; where were you?"—his tone suggesting that Luis couldn't keep track of his wife. Luis was infuriated and embarrassed. He had been raised in a culture where the man goes out and the woman faithfully has a hot meal ready for him when he gets back. That's how the marriages worked that he had observed as he grew up. So when Maria began to rebel, he found himself powerless to regain control. Then came the night of the big blowup when Maria sped off in the car . . .

Luis stumbled back into the house and slouched on the sofa. The TV was on—as usual—but this time he couldn't lose himself in its flickering action or enticing commercials. His mind kept going over their fight and the memory of kicking Maria. He'd never done that before. *To kick a woman . . . that was really low. I must be losing it!*

Slowly Luis began to ask himself some hard questions: *What went wrong? How could this have happened?* It had been so long, so very long since they had really talked to each other. "In the

past," recalls Luis, "I could always pac-
ify Maria with a sincere promise to do
better or with a gift and some flowers.
But this was different." He knew that
this blowup was bigger than his charm
or promises or gifts of atonement could
handle. They'd lost control of their marriage, and for the first time Luis really
started to worry that they were slipping
toward a divorce without even a straw
to grasp to slow things down. Luis
wanted to call a time-out and regroup,
but the chance seemed to have passed
him by.

*Maria and Luis are in a bind. They don't
know how to deal with their anger and
pain. They now understand more fully
who they are and how they can hurt each
other, but this makes closeness dangerous.
In fact, closeness has turned abusive, and
whenever they are together the air is filled
with tension. They've discovered that if
they come too close, they're like a flame
and gunpowder—explosive. Not knowing
what else to do, they settle into a cold war
with neutral zones and boundaries. With
each of them seeking more autonomy and*

time apart, a predictable level of isolation and loneliness begins.

Couples caught in a desperate, futile attempt to keep on looking good—even though they can hardly be in the same room together—put a tremendous strain on themselves and all those around them. Children looking for security find uncertainty and even danger. Other family and friends wanting to help face bewilderment. A multitude of anxious, angry, and intense vibrations encircle the relationship, and everyone connected feels the pain.

In the days that followed, Luis began battling a new emotion: tremendous rejection. He felt terrible that Maria saw him as someone to run away from, trying to escape some sort of monster. The feeling of rejection created a growing depression, like a black cloud hanging over his home.

Then he found out that there *was* another man in Maria's life. Depression gave way to a seething anger. He considered Maria's friends his enemies, and the battle lines were drawn. His first countermove was to see a lawyer about filing for a divorce. He'd get even; he'd get custody of the children and make her pay. Hatred and jealousy consumed his waking thoughts and haunted his dreams. Feelings of rage and murderous retaliation rolled over and over in his mind.

But in the middle of it all Luis's heart was breaking and crumbling. He spent endless nights driving around town searching for Maria. Deep down he just wanted his wife and marriage back. He wanted some relief from all the emotions that hung on him from the time he got up in the morning until he found a brief relief in sleep at night.

Too often sleep wouldn't come. Alone at home with the children, Luis would envision Maria out partying with her friends, having a good time running from club to club, or possibly sharing an intimate evening with another man. Luis had been the only man Maria had ever known; now that was shattered. How could she do it?

The only bright spot in Luis's life was his kids. At least he had Juan and Theresa, and so he threw his whole energy into their care. He cooked and did laundry and read stories and tucked them into bed. But even that was tarnished with resentment; he felt cheated that he had to bear all the responsibilities for raising them while Maria was out partying.

As Luis started to rebuild his life around his children, he began to withdraw from other people. "My kids seemed the only ones I could trust," recalls Luis. "They always supported me, never argued with me; they seemed to be the only ones loyal to me."

Luis had been drinking alcohol since he was fourteen years old, when he had stolen a fifth of brandy from his dad. But as the weeks went by after the terrible fight with Maria, he began to purposefully stay numbed with alcohol. Whenever the kids were with their mother he would stop after work and buy a half-pint of bourbon or rum and a two-liter bottle of Coke, then just sit at home, watch television, and quietly get drunk.

He was slipping deeper and deeper into depression. He often woke up in the morning on the couch with the television on and an empty bottle of liquor and an ashtray full of cigarette butts on the table beside him. But he was careful not to drink in front of his children; to them he wanted to appear strong. He felt there had to be at least one stable force in their lives, but it was difficult because inside he was falling apart.

Then one night he made the mistake of drinking while they were at home. "After a while," he says, "I took them in my arms and tried to explain to them what was happening to our family. I started to cry uncontrollably on their shoulders. I never before felt so tired and defeated in my life. I needed desperately to unload on someone, anyone other than an eight-year-old and a two-year-old. But there was no one. I was alone."

We need to relate to stay alive. To touch and be touched. To hear and be heard. To love and be loved. These are necessary for existence. That's how we were created. That's how we are. To be alone and lonely brings on despair. Interests fade, activities narrow, the body disrupts its normal patterns, and pain swallows us up. Any re-

*lief—no matter how destructive or inef-
fective in the long term—is desired. Des-
peration and despair block honesty and
openness because of internal messages
that go along with them. Such thinking as
"I'm getting what I deserve" or "nobody
cares anyway" only contributes to shut-
ting down communication. No help
sought, no help received—a vicious down-
ward spiral of hopelessness gains momen-
tum.*

To make matters worse—if they ever
could be—the sawmill where Luis
worked went out on strike when con-
tract negotiations broke off. So on top of
everything else he was out of a job, too.
Because he was on strike, he couldn't
draw unemployment. His only income
was $60 a week from the strike fund,
and that wasn't enough to pay the rent
on the house, so he had to move into
something cheaper. The bulk of the furniture was placed in storage, and Luis
and the kids found themselves living in
an upstairs studio apartment. Possibly
the only good thing to come out of
being out of work was that Luis didn't

have the money to pursue the divorce any further.

Finally, to ease his loneliness, Luis began inviting people over to the tiny apartment. Some came over just to party, and guys often used his apartment to crash for a night or two; Luis was always throwing out trash cans full of whiskey bottles and cigarette butts. He didn't like the atmosphere for the children, but it helped ease his sense of isolation. Among the guys from work who dropped by, however, were some Christians. Luis found their outlook on life to be refreshing, and their concern for him seemed real, not phony. They reminded Luis of Alicia and Roger, Maria's sister and brother-in-law.

Alicia and Roger, who were also Christians, had been spending time with Luis and Maria in the months before they separated. Alicia and Roger had often come over and tried to talk about God. At the time, Maria didn't want to have anything to do with religion. She said that Alicia and Roger always seemed to be preaching to her—even if they didn't say anything.

But Luis had found something about them attractive . . . even if they always seemed to arrive when Luis and Maria were in the middle of an embarrassing fight.

And now the Christian guys who sometimes dropped by Luis's apartment also seemed to have some answers that he was looking for—happiness, assurance, and a feeling of belonging. "They told me of the love God had for me," Luis recalls. "They shared their own experiences and prayed with me, and somehow that eased some of the hatred that was burning inside me. Slowly I started feeling that maybe there was hope, but I had no idea how to grasp it."

Then one day as Maria was dropping the kids off, Luis was heading for the grocery store. He invited her to go along. "To my surprise she agreed to come," remembers Luis. "We talked about each other's 'separate' futures, and I noticed a hint of remorse and indecision in her conversation. I got bold and told Maria I loved her still, and we embraced somewhat clumsily in the aisle of the store. Suddenly that glimmer of hope seemed to have substance." As a direct result of Luis's contact with his new Christian friends, some of the hostility that was burning inside of him was starting to subside.

Being around authentic Christians provided Luis with a model of openness and acceptance. What better place to take the risk of openness than with God? Being loved by God doesn't require looking good. Christian fellowship encourages one to seek a deeper set of friendships. Like a mountain climber slipping down the face of a cliff, Luis searched for solid footing. Looking good had slipped away, booze no longer worked, the children were not strong enough to give him what he needed, his wife was unreachable. Perhaps through Christian friends—maybe, just maybe—something could be found.

One of the times we are most open to new ideas is when we feel we have tried everything. If we can keep from becoming totally cynical or apathetic, opportunity may be revealed. Being around people who have healthier relationships at a time when we are lost and searching can be very helpful. For Luis, it provided him the time to test some of his assumptions. Is it the husband's job to control his wife? Maybe not. Must he live a life in which he is never forgiven and never forgives? Maybe not. Is there a positive way of living after the attempts to look perfect have failed? Maybe so!

Maria and Luis had now been separated about four months, and she was again living at her parents' home. Luis felt Maria's parents' home was neutral ground—a place apart from her old friends whom he resented so much. Also, he had always gotten along well with Maria's parents and knew that they weren't blaming anyone for the problems. They just wanted Luis and Maria back together. "I found myself spending a lot of time over there," recalls Luis. "Juan was out of school for the summer, and Maria had the kids. Their home was in the country, and it was a relaxed atmosphere. We were at least being civil toward one another. We would spend Sundays at the park or the movies, but I had this unsettled feeling that what little peace we had could erupt into fighting or arguing or even physical violence at any moment. We seemed to do all right as long as we didn't spend too much time together. But that wasn't being a family."

Luis was realizing that he really was a family man—that's what he wanted. So he asked Maria to move back in with him. She knew it was a risk, but she agreed. They all crammed into the little studio apartment. They lived nearly on top of each other. There was no room to maneuver emotionally or physically. It was a bad time and no way to launch the delicate venture of trying to get back together. Arguments broke out from day one.

But the strike at Luis's work had finally been resolved, and so with the increased income, they rented a little two-bedroom house. This was better, but while desire is essential to solve problems, success requires much more. The first time Luis got so angry that he put his fist through the wall, Maria gave up. Maybe this was all there was to marriage. Maybe they would always be fighting. Luis said he was sorry and promised never to lose his temper again, but Maria wasn't buying any of that. He had made and broken so many promises, what good were more apologies and promises?

Within a few short weeks things seemed as bad as they had ever been. Then one night Maria's brother-in-law, Roger, dropped by to see Luis. Luis told him how tired he was of trying to make their marriage work. He felt like giving up. It seemed like he and Maria were always walking on eggshells when they were around each other, and when one of the shells broke, well, it sure made a mess, not an omelet. Luis confessed that it really wasn't working. They still never really talked together, and he still felt a lot of jealousy and hurt. He really couldn't forgive Maria. And try as he would, when all the old ghosts would pop up, he'd lose control. And if he didn't end up hitting Maria, some piece of furniture was sure to be broken, especially if he had been drinking.

Then Roger opened his Bible and began to share some Scriptures with Luis about forgiveness. They talked first about how God wanted to forgive Luis, and then how he could begin to forgive Maria really deep down so those feelings of resentment wouldn't be there any more to resurface. It was a Monday night, and Luis had been watching Pete Rose in one of his long hitting streaks. But what Roger was saying began to get through to Luis in spite of the murmur of the Cincinnati ball game on TV. "I felt at the end of my rope and decided to try," remembers Luis. "We prayed together, and at Roger's urging, I asked the Lord into my life. I hardly knew what I was doing, and I was half-distracted by the TV, but somehow the Lord honored my little venture of faith.

"Roger invited me to attend church with his family that following Sunday. Roger and Alicia seemed to have such a solid marriage that I began to think this new way might lead to some help. So I agreed to go."

To Luis's great surprise on Sunday morning, Maria began dressing for church also. Luis didn't say anything but just took her and the kids along as though it was what they always did on a Sunday morning.

Maria had been realizing that something was missing from her life, and she had tried to make some external adjustments—cutting down on the drinking and running around. "Even before I had moved back in with Luis I had become disillusioned with my life," she says. "The people I'd met were all just out for a good time. No one really cared about me. I would drink until I was intoxicated and could feel no pain . . . but I still missed Luis. Even while I was living with my parents I decided that I still loved him. But my feelings were very mixed; one day I would feel love for him, and the next I felt nothing but pity. I had wanted the best of both worlds. I wanted Luis, and I also wanted my freedom. But slowly I was realizing that I had to make a choice. I knew there was nothing worthwhile in the path of partying all the time."

But moving back in with Luis and the kids hadn't proved to be the answer either. Things had become as bad as they had ever been. But that week after

Roger had come over somehow seemed different.

"Luis tried to talk to me. He was trying to make me believe that we could make our marriage work. But even though he seemed very tender and loving in a new way, I didn't have any hope. How could it work? In the past he would always promise to change, but he never did. However, this time I knew that my brother-in-law, Roger, had been talking to Luis—and when Roger talked, it always got around to God. And I recognized that something was happening in Luis's heart. He *was* changing. So when Luis told me that he was going to church with Roger and Alicia, I decided to go too."

At church that morning Maria heard an old friend sing a song that really hit home with her. The song was titled "I Needed Him," and it almost told the story of her life—how for her whole life she had been searching for something and didn't know it was Jesus. When the service was over, the pastor gave an altar call, and Maria went down to the front. Roger then grabbed Luis's arm and said,

"Come on! Go pray with your wife."
Kneeling beside Maria, Luis realized his
wife was really crying.

In all their married life Luis had seldom seen Maria cry, even though he had
sometimes treated her terribly. So when
he saw her sobbing her heart out, it
really touched him. "She seemed so vulnerable to me," he says. "Somehow I
knew she was really sorry for everything
that had happened, and it really soft-
ened my heart toward her. I think that
was the first time I had really taken a
good look at my wife and realized some
of the damage I had done to her."

That insight further changed Luis.
He, too, began to repent for how he had
treated Maria, and this time it went far
deeper than his former feeble apologies
and hollow promises to change. "I
know it sounds too simple," he says,
"but when we gave our lives to Jesus,
our marriage began to turn around."

Experiencing God's forgiveness
helped Luis begin to understand what it
meant to forgive Maria. It didn't happen
all at once, but Maria says, "Luis's atti-
tude toward me began to change. He

was less bitter, and he quit throwing my past life up to me. He also quit drinking. As these changes happened, Jesus has enabled me to put it all behind, to overcome all the hurt and guilt that I had bottled up inside.

"It hasn't been easy," continues Maria. "We still have our everyday struggles, but I've opened my heart, and I am more willing to take that extra step. Jesus has filled the void in my life that I had always tried to fill with other things. He's changed my desires."

Finally, Luis and Maria started really communicating. They started communicating first with Jesus. Building a relationship with their Creator and Sustainer provided the model and foundation upon which their marital communication could be helped. There was no need to try to fool God. God already knew and loved them still. Talking with Jesus provided a new direction, a new way out. Closeness and acceptance did not need to be built on feeble attempts to look good. Instead, the wounded, scared, and angry parts of their lives could be shared, understood, and nurtured.

Because God risked loving them, they could risk loving each other . . . just as they were. The risk of forgiving each other seemed much more attainable because God had shown the way. He had forgiven them even before they became aware of their individual guilt.

Not only did this freedom from guilt and resentment break down the most significant barriers between them, but as Luis and Maria began to discover that sharing one's pain with Jesus did not result in ridicule or rejection, it relieved some of their most powerful and long-standing fears. Communication with Jesus provides opportunities to test our fears and to receive the power to be vulnerable with our spouse. Having received a response of forgiveness, caring, and encouragement on a spiritual level empowers the Christian couple to do likewise.

In addition, Maria and Luis received a new focus for their family life. It was not their feeble attempts to look good to others or to escape being near each other; now they could focus on serving the Lord. This *provided a powerfully unifying force for their family's life. As a Christian couple they could place their marriage under God's authority.*

Roger and Alicia became even more involved with Luis and Maria. The two couples began to have a weekly Bible study together. Roger and Alicia loaned them a Bible because Luis and Maria didn't have one. And as Luis and Maria began to get involved in church activities, they developed a new circle of friends—together this time.

But best of all, Luis feels that the fear of things exploding has become less and less of a threat. And that's something that the children notice. Luis remembers one Sunday morning when his family was in the car waiting for him. He was the last to leave the house, and as he was closing the front door, he turned to look into the living room. "I saw the scars of all the battles that Maria and I had fought; they were to remain there as memories. But in the center of the room, I felt the radiating peace of God. He had truly come into our home.

There has grown in our family a feeling of security that only a strong family love can bring."

It is no longer necessary for Juan to protectively herd Theresa into another room to find a place of physical safety. Luis and Maria still disagree on things, but they have boundary lines that God has helped them put up, and He has helped them not to cross those boundaries.

One of the practical things that Maria and Luis have had to work hard on is developing a unified approach to their children. Maria felt that their children received no discipline unless she provided it. "Luis was raised in such an easy-going style that our own kids could be going nuts, and he would just sit there as though nothing were happening." Sometimes they still disagree on what's good for the kids, but they've worked hard to come to a more balanced approach to their children.

It's largely because the deep wells of guilt and resentment have been drained that Luis and Maria can now communicate and discuss their problems so much better. "I don't feel like I have to keep my feelings pressed down inside me anymore," says Maria. "We do things together. We also share friends and try not to let them come between us. We are enjoying each other now in ways we never did. We also have family time during which we pray together."

A marriage enrichment weekend was very helpful for Luis and Maria in building better communication skills. This was one of the first times Maria had been able to open up and share about her feelings. It felt to her like a risk to do it, but in that supportive setting, Luis learned much more about what she needed to make their relationship fulfilling to her.

Once hope is revived, couples who were previously struggling merely to survive can redirect their energies toward growth. People have been trying to figure out marriage for a long, long time. And some important lessons have been learned. For instance, most couples develop a style of conflict in their communication. When this style is discovered, the couple can *often make adjustments to reach a better outcome. Marriage counselor Norm Wright, in his book* The Pillars of Marriage, *suggests five ways husbands and wives have of dealing with differences.*[*]

1. Withdrawal. *Conflict is not worth the effort, especially if previous experience with conflict proved negative.*
2. Winning. *Winning or proving your point becomes the major objective.*
3. Yielding. *We all must yield sometimes, but yielding can be a means of protecting oneself. Anger, however, piles up and eventually comes out.*
4. Compromise. *Though this sounds good, it is based on giving a little to get a little. Unfortunately, there often remains resentment over what was lost.*
5. Resolve. *This starts with direct, loving communication. Each person tells needs and feelings. There is no attacking or judgment of the other. Though yielding or compromise will sometimes result, the understanding*

---

[*]H. Norman Wright, *The Pillars of Marriage* (Ventura, Calif.: Regal Books, 1979), pp. 147-148.

sought in this approach ideally helps the parties through mutual agreement on the resolution.

Helping their marriage grow is still hard work for Maria and Luis, but they feel it is worth the effort. Maria remembers a very dear friend telling her that if she would put Jesus first in her life, she could have the marriage and love that she had always yearned for. It was hard to believe at the time, but God has restored her love for Luis. "We are at peace now," she says, "and we thank the Lord every day for coming into our lives. We now have hope. We have Jesus Christ."

With their marriage on the right track, Maria and Luis were especially delighted with two additions to their family—one planned and one a surprise. Says Maria, "God gave us Robbi and Elissa as gifts to complete our family."

CHAPTER THREE

Intimate Strangers

Les Baxter shrugged on his jacket, threw his toolbox in the back of the pickup, and slid his six-foot-three-inch frame into the cab. As he turned the key and glanced over the gauges, he frowned. Fuel tank: empty.

Les hit the steering wheel with his hand and swore under his breath. Sixteen-year-old Laura had taken the pickup out last night and—once again—didn't think to put in any gas. Now he was going to have to fill up on the way to work . . . if he didn't go dry on the highway first.

When Les got home that night he went right to the kitchen to talk to his wife about Laura. He and Andrea had only been married two years, and Les had learned fast that it never worked to confront his stepchildren without first working it out with their mother.

Gary, age ten, was sprawled at the kitchen table stuffing a sandwich into his mouth. "You're going to spoil your dinner, Gary," Les said automatically. "Look, I've got to talk to your mom about something, so bug off, OK?"

Gary grabbed the other half of his sandwich and sauntered off. Les felt a familiar irritation but decided to let it pass.

"Andrea," he plunged right in, "Laura used the pickup last night and left the tank empty—again. That's the fourth time she's used the truck this week, and she never puts in any gas! We've really got to do something about it!"

Andrea looked annoyed. "You're the one who wanted her to get her license so we didn't have to drive her everywhere."

"That's not the point!" said Les. "I just don't think she has to leave the tank empty!"

His wife jerked open the refrigerator and took out lettuce, a cucumber, and some green onions. "Can't we talk about this some other time? I just got home from work a half hour ago, and I've got to get supper."

Les took the lettuce from her and started tearing it into the salad bowl. "You always want to talk about this 'another time.' It doesn't have to be a big deal—let's just lay down the law or work out some plan so I don't run out of gas on my way to work in the morning!"

"Don't get so mad at Laura." Andrea's eyes brimmed as she chopped the cucumber. "I should have told her to check the gas and given her money before she went out last night."

Les stared at his wife. "Andrea, it's not *your* fault, for crying out loud. Why can't we just tell her if she wants to use the truck, she has to put gas in it?"

"Why do you always pick on the kids?" Andrea shot back. "You pick on Gary for eating a sandwich . . . you pick on Laura because she forgot to fill the gas tank. They're only kids, Les!"

"What's that supposed to mean? We let Gary eat twenty minutes before supper and ruin his appetite? We let Laura use up all the gas? Of course they're kids, but they've got to learn responsibility!" He was in danger of losing his temper.

"You don't have to get so angry!" Andrea cried. "Laura's a responsible driver. She always asks to use the pickup. Why are you so hard on her?" Andrea dropped the paring knife and cucumber and rushed from the room.

Les shook his head as if to clear tangled cobwebs. What had just happened? Why was this such a big deal? It had seemed so simple to him; all he wanted was for Laura to put gas in the truck when she used it. Was that expecting too much?

Les Baxter, dark-haired and bearded, had worked for a national tire company as a mechanic for fifteen years. When he first met Andrea, a bookkeeper with the same company, he didn't seem fazed that she had been married twice before and had two kids. She was petite and attractive, with honey-colored wisps framing her face. They seemed to have a lot in common—both loved to read, enjoyed camping, and had a yen to travel. Both had grown up Catholic and attended parochial schools. They fell in love and decided to get married—her third time, his first.

"I married a whole family, not just a wife," Les says. Laura was fourteen at the time; Gary was eight. "I had no problem with a ready-made family. But I was raised as an only child by just my mom. The role of 'father' was unclear to me, and suddenly I was one! I felt unsure. I knew the kids needed more direction and discipline; however, when I tried to make suggestions, I received a lot of static from Andrea. I felt that she over-compensated with the kids, trying to make up for previous mistakes."

Andrea had been surprised when she fell in love with Les Baxter. Years before—at sixteen—she had gotten pregnant and married the father of her baby girl. He turned out to be an alcoholic, and later, after they had another child, he abandoned the family. At age twenty-five, with two children, Andrea tried again. Her second husband, a drug addict, was abusive. At thirty she felt like a two-time loser on her way to the altar again, this time with Les. The heroines of the romantic novels she read bounced back from incredible problems and lived happily ever after. Maybe it would happen for her.

"But even after I married Les," Andrea says, "I felt very lonely. I was afraid I'd get hurt again. The thought of failing in marriage tore me up inside. I got sick; I had headaches and other physical problems, but I kept silent about my fears."

Few marriages begin with challenges as big as those that face stepfamilies. Divided loyalties, different and sometimes unknown histories and habits, and lots and lots of complicated relationships characterize marriages with children from previous relationships. Les faced instant fatherhood, a task for which, for better or worse, he had no role model—not even his own dad. He had no fathering experience of any kind. Andrea also brought her challenges in the form of deep hurt, guilt, and fear from two failed marriages.

While divorces and multiple marriages are not an ideal, in our society they are a

*reality. And blended families have addi-
tional challenges that need especially good
communication between husband and wife
and between parents and children. Unfortunately, persons who marry for a second
time typically have difficulty talking about
the fears and frustrations they face, especially where children are involved.*

Looking back, Les says, "I really stumbled into marriage blind. I thought I
knew what it was all about, but half-
grown children complicated things. I
had my own ideas on discipline, having
grown up in a fairly strict household.
Andrea's discipline, on the other hand,
seemed lax and uneven to me, and I felt
the children were taking advantage of it."

Les decided that the Baxter household had to have a boss, and it was *not*
going to be the kids. But when he tried
to act as he thought a father should, he
and Andrea got into a fight. "I went
about setting up what I thought were
good rules and regulations for the kids
to follow, determining not to let them
walk all over me as I felt they were doing
to their mother. But every time I tried to

lower the boom, there was Andrea telling me I was being unfair or that I didn't love her or the kids!"

It took Les a while to figure out what was going wrong. "Andrea seemed conditioned to think that whenever the male of the house got mad, all hell might break loose. She was unable to believe I was any different from her other two husbands, and she wouldn't let me prove myself, even though I felt I had done nothing to justify her fears. I felt guilty till proven innocent. But every time I tried to talk to Andrea about it, I ran into a brick wall."

Andrea admits that the wall between them was already there when they first got married. "I didn't trust Les because of my previous husbands, who were unpredictable and abusive. Les didn't appear real. I kept wondering when he would blow it, when he would whip my kids."

Part of her sensed the bind her new husband was in. "I felt caught in the middle between Les and the kids. At the same time, I was disappointed in myself. I couldn't control my fear and mistrust. Guilt played a big role when Les disciplined the kids. I would panic. I was afraid the kids would blame me. Even though I knew the kids were in the wrong, my past experience would block that out, and I would step in between Les and the kids. I couldn't let them be hurt anymore because of me. As always, I shifted the blame onto myself. The kids knew this and took advantage of my feelings."

Typical interchanges went something like this:

"Laura! Gary! You were both given chores to do this weekend. Why is the trash still sitting there? And your rooms haven't been cleaned. You both better do those chores *now*, or there's going to be trouble!"

"Les, wait a minute," Andrea would intercede. "Gary asked if he could play basketball, and I let him. And Laura was helping me with this special recipe I was trying out."

"Andrea, I *told* Gary he couldn't play basketball until his chores were done. He's just trying to get out of doing what he's supposed to do by getting us to disagree."

"I can't do my chores now!" Laura wailed. "I have plans this evening."

"That's right, Les. She and—"

"Andrea! Quit letting her off the hook! She's not going anywhere till she finishes those chores."

Laura whirled on her mother. "He's not my father. He can't tell me what to do. You're my mother; only you can say what I should or shouldn't do."

Andrea looked like a frightened rabbit caught in a trap. "Now, Laura, it's his house too. He has a right to expect you children to obey him."

"Well, it's my home too. Don't I have any rights?"

"Yeah, Mom," Gary chimed in.

"You said I could go tonight, Mom, so I'm going!" Laura flounced from the room. Gary glided out in her wake.

"Now look what you've done, Andrea!"

"Me? All you care about is your rules. You don't really care about the kids—or me, for that matter! You just want to be the big boss around here! Everything was fine until you came in here like a macho policeman. Give the kids a break. The stupid chores can wait till tomorrow."

"Andrea—"

"I don't want to talk about it any more!" Andrea turned and walked out of the room.

Les stared after his retreating family, then shook his head in frustration. Why did it always go so wrong? Later that evening he thought about trying to work something out with Andrea. But his wife had her nose in a book and seemed unreachable.

Raising a teenager has plenty of challenges. Parents constantly worry: Are we being too lenient or too strict? As Andrea's guilt regarding her daughter's disrupted childhood silently ate away at her, she tried to "protect" her. But the guilt feelings went unspoken and therefore unresolved. "Protection" resulted in being manipulated. Neither Les nor Andrea saw Laura through the other's eyes. Andrea didn't hear Les's concerns about the dangers of an unstructured youth. Les didn't hear

Andrea's concerns that they not be too harsh on top of Laura's already difficult childhood. The most painful of all was that neither heard each other's hopes for Laura to have a wonderful life. All of this was because of a lack of good communication.

After one such bout over the kids, Andrea threatened to leave. Les was shocked! "Andrea's actions didn't seem in line with our quarrel. Sure, we were having some rough times, but it didn't feel like anything major. I didn't understand her reaction and was confused—especially since we had been married only a short time and I thought of us as still being on our honeymoon. Inside I felt lost, thinking what a mistake I had made giving up my freedom for *this*.

"Part of my frustration," Les continues, "was that I felt there was no way to talk about these things with Andrea, no way of working them out. It was like knocking on the door with nobody answering. There was a part of her I wasn't able to know or see."

Although the most obvious area of

tension was discipline of the kids, Andrea admits their communication problems spilled over into other areas. "I avoided arguments. I would read books and ignore Les. Instead of talking things out, I buried problems inside. When we did talk, it was mostly about practical concerns or work or other people, not ourselves."

Les says they were "intimate strangers" during those first two years of marriage. "When I'd feel frustrated over some unresolved problem, I'd think, *Guess it's best to leave this area alone for the sake of harmony.* There was no honest sharing between us. We joked that the honeymoon was over! But it was no joke."

By leaving this or that area alone "for the sake of harmony," Les thought he was putting the problem out of his mind. But all he really did was bury the problem in the back of his mind where it grew. When the next blowup came, he and Andrea would fight about not only the new problem but also all the old ones that resurfaced.

Andrea's frustration was also building. "I felt as if I was being torn in two emotionally. Pulled to the breaking point between the kids and Les, I would finally lash out at Les saying, 'You hate my kids!' Or even, 'I can't take this anymore! I'm going to leave!' In fact, I snapped at everyone in the family. The only place I felt safe was at work."

Despite her religious upbringing, Andrea didn't even know how to talk with God anymore. "I felt totally separated from Him. I didn't think He could help. This was a very gray time in my life. I was on an island by myself in a storm. I was frightened and didn't know what to do to help myself."

Like many people, Les thought he could just let things go for the sake of harmony, but in reality he was just stuffing them down inside. Stuffing down problems doesn't make them go away. And the next time they resurface, the frustrations and disagreements make the blowup all the bigger.

Andrea's fears from past relationships kept her from talking about areas of disagreement. It never occurred to her that disagreements could be resolved. Her automatic response was to shut off the dialogue if an issue came up—or just avoid it in the first place. Talking about noncontroversial things, or keeping herself unavailable by hiding behind her books or hobbies, became a well-worn pattern.

Communication is risky business. Knowing good ways to state your thoughts and being a keen listener helps. But skilled communication doesn't remove the step of faith that must be taken. Sharing a different opinion may cause an unresolvable conflict. When hurt is expressed, anger, pity, or ridicule may result. Exposed weakness may elicit fear, such as fear of being controlled, being pushed too hard, or being given up on.

Every interaction before marriage provides each person with information about how the other will respond. Les and Andrea couldn't communicate well with each other, but it wasn't because they didn't want to. The origin of their struggles was in what they had learned in their past. Our fears, beliefs, and self-perceptions start early in life. To the extent that we don't recognize what fears and beliefs influence us, their affects linger deeply within to control us.

If you were to step inside either Les's or Andrea's mind for a moment, you would be able to hear their self talk: "That really hurt." "That's not even worth mentioning." "If anyone ever found out that about me, they wouldn't like me." "Nobody can ever understand; nobody ever does." "Just do what you are told and keep your mouth shut." And the list goes on. In fact, their list isn't much different from yours and mine, and it sure makes marriage tough.

Other differences between Andrea and Les nibbled at the edges of their strained relationship. Both enjoy reading. But Les leans toward science fiction—a definite "Star Trek" fan. Action! Solving problems! Moving forward! No world is too tough to conquer! Andrea, on the other hand, likes romance novels. "She has this ideal of her knight in shining armor," Les says wryly. "I'm afraid my armor is a little tarnished."

Andrea recalls that when they were dating, Les called regularly; he even sent a plant once. The calls stopped after they were married. "I would have loved getting calls from work or flowers occasionally. But he'd say he didn't know what to get me for my birthday or anniversary and tell me to go pick something out. That hurt. So I buried myself in my novels; I wanted romance in my life.

Les admits he's not a very romantic person. "I can't see buying flowers, spending good money for something that will be tossed out in a few days. A plant that will live on is OK, but you've only got so much room for plants before they crowd you out of the house. So I tend to be more practical when it comes to presents. Also," he admits with a shrug, "I'm lazy and don't like to shop."

Unfortunately, Andrea took Les's lack of romance to mean that he didn't really love her; and if he didn't love her, then maybe he would be like the others and do a Jekyll-and-Hyde.

Even though Andrea often cut off communication when she felt threatened, she wanted Les to talk. "I wanted Les to share part of himself with me. If he was open with me, maybe I could trust him a little more and share some of my feelings with him. I wanted to let him know that I was hurting, that I had been scarred not only physically in the past, but emotionally too. I wanted to test the waters and hear him tell me why kids should be disciplined in certain areas. What did he think would be the end result of this discipline? Would the children respect him more and grow to love him? If so, why?"

Les wanted to talk—when there was a problem to be handled. "At times I tried to discuss things with Andrea, tried to delve into our problems to clear them away, but I always ran into the brick wall. She didn't trust me and wouldn't open up to me. Only later did I understand that she thought if she did, I would use her fears against her."

Andrea's past always seemed to intrude. "When I was married to the kids' father," she recalls, "he began to drink more and more. He would become angry and abuse us verbally, physically, and emotionally. I didn't know how long I could last in this situation or what it was doing to the kids. But I was afraid I couldn't make it on my own and take care of two children."

Her second marriage was on the rebound from the first. "What I thought was a strong man turned out to be a bully. I had done it again!" Andrea says regretfully. "I now had no trust in my judgment of people. When I finally married Les, I was afraid the same thing was going to happen all over again. I kept waiting for Les to turn into a monster who would abuse me or the kids. I remember wondering if he knew or sensed these feelings in me. I was afraid I might end up alone again for the third time with the kids. So I kept on reading romances that ended happily ever after."

Unfortunately neither Andrea nor Les had anyone to confide in. "My mother would say, 'What have you done now?'" says Andrea. "No way was I going to talk to her! And I was too proud to share my fears with friends. People thought we had this perfectly great marriage, and that is all I wanted them to know. And Les and I weren't talking to each other about anything personal. So

I just kept reacting to particular situations as they came up."

Les also felt he had nowhere to turn for help. His family was distant, and all his old friends were single—no help there. At that time the Baxters weren't going to church, so they didn't look there either.

Misunderstandings are painful. Saying, "I care; I'm connected to you; I value your life as much as my own," makes us vulnerable. We go out on a limb every time we try to say those kinds of things to one another. And if our attempts to express care and love go unnoticed or are rejected, it can be downright traumatic.

Successfully expressing love isn't as easy as it appears in the movies. Each partner's unique "language" of love must be learned. Spouses often fail to communicate their love, not because they don't try, but because they use a language their partner doesn't understand. Before a loving statement is received, it must be interpreted by the receiver as loving. The old adage, "It's the thought that counts," is not enough in love. Why? Because it doesn't register in a way that benefits the relationship until the other person receives and understands the message. And that usually requires good timing and clear communication.

We come into marriage knowing some of how we want to be loved. And we've usually had a little experience trying to express love to others within our family and circle of friends. But marriage tests us more than any other relationship. We want so much; our spouse wants so much. Les and Andrea were giving what they imagined the other person wanted. Les's approach was practical; he wanted to deal with a specific problem. But this was threatening to Andrea; she wanted to get to know Les first apart from a crisis, to see whether he was someone she could trust in the first place. Because they were unable to discuss their needs and desires in a helpful way, they were unsuccessful in communicating their love to one another. Without a lifetime of communication practice, we miss many of the chances to love.

We all have a very personal set of behaviors that we consider to be loving. The other person's emotions of love are not very easily recognized, and even some behaviors don't work either. For instance, just because a wife enjoys having her head rubbed doesn't necessarily mean her husband will recognize that she is expressing love if she rubs his head while he's watching a football game. All her good intentions would receive little appreciation. Her husband might think she was seeing if his hair was clean or simply messing it up without thinking. On the other hand, if he were to give her a head rub—which he might seldom think of doing—she would purr like a kitten and be reminded that he loved her very much.

For Les, resolving practical problems was the way he thought he could show love to Andrea . . . because that's what he would appreciate. But for Andrea, expressions of feelings and tokens of romance were what she longed for.

When spouses can't communicate well, the ordinary problems of life (such as how to discipline the kids) loom larger and larger. Disappointments go uncared for, and life sinks into despair. Not only is the ideal of marriage long forgotten, but mere emotional survival can feel tenuous. Fortunately for Les and Andrea, they took a person. More often than not, Gary would refer to him as 'my dad.'"

The more Andrea wrote down her feelings, the more hope she began to feel. "I knew we were on the right road to make our marriage stronger and more trusting. I also knew it wouldn't be easy. I was leaving myself wide open to be hurt again. But the thought of Les being dead and never seeing him again was more painful than any other hurt I've experienced. Life would be too empty to bear. The tears kept falling; I didn't think they were ever going to stop."

Les came back to their room, and they read each other's letters. By the time they had finished, both were crying together. "Why didn't we recognize the depth of our feelings for each other before this?" Les wonders. "I guess the everyday struggle to make ends meet and all the other frustrations of adjusting to marriage kept getting in our way."

What was so important about that Marriage Encounter? "I felt hope that weekend," Les says. "I felt excitement. I got to see some of the hidden part of

step that eventually opened a door to hope for their marriage.

The Baxters, both raised Catholic, had not been attending church. But one Sunday they decided to go, for no particular reason . . . "except God must have been trying to shove us in the right direction!" said Les, laughing. As they entered the back of church, he stopped at the bulletin board and saw an invitation to a couples' party. He pointed it out to Andrea, and they decided it might be fun to meet some couples since their circle of friends was rather small.

When Les and Andrea arrived at the address on the invitation and met their hosts, the two couples were attracted to each other from the start. Their friendship grew until they became close friends.

A short time later their new friends invited Les and Andrea over to share something with them. "When we arrived," Les recalls, "I could tell that something was different—they were so alive and bubbly. Then they told us about the past weekend when they had been to a Marriage Encounter. I thought, *How nice.*"

Their new friends couldn't recommend this experience enough. "Les and Andrea, you really should go. You'll never regret it! It meant a lot to us and really put some new life in our marriage."

"OK," Les stalled, "sometime we will." Six months later their friends were still insisting they should go—and saying they would pay for it.

"We should probably go," Andrea pointed out to Les. "They're our best friends now, and we don't want to hurt their feelings."

Les agreed, but he wasn't looking forward to it. He managed to get a Saturday off and reluctantly went, even though he could think of a hundred other things he'd rather do with a day off.

The Baxters arrived on Friday night, checked in, and went to the first talk. "We listened to speakers tell us how we could make a good marriage even better," Les says. "At first I just pretended to get involved. But after listening to what was being said through Saturday

and into Sunday, things began
through to me about how to reall
municate with each other."

"The Marriage Encounter we
started me thinking that it was un
keep part of me secret," says Andi
admitted I didn't trust my husba
was afraid sharing would give him
munition against me. But I decic
had to open up and be vulnerab
cried a lot. Many of the couples c
with us."

Sunday afternoon arrived, the f
session. The couples were told to w
a letter to each other on what it wo
be like if their partner was no lor
there. "I was trying to answer the qu
tion, What would I feel if Les die
Andrea remembers. "The tears drip
off my face as I wrote down what I
I knew then that nothing in the
could touch what Les and I hac
gether. I realized he was everyth
wanted in a husband for myself a
father for my children. The que
opened my eyes. The kids reall
respect him. They were not really
of him. They really did care for hi

Andrea, and it was like finding out I married a different person. Our masks slipped down quite a bit."

Les pauses, thinking back to the turning point. "We were talking without fighting for the first time. I had doubts that she loved me; I learned that we did love each other. When I tried to really listen to Andrea, it seemed to break down her fears. It took awhile, but that weekend they began to crumble. And," he adds, "we allowed God to come into our marriage."

Hope-filled living doesn't wait for all the challenges of life to be solved and all the battles to be won. A loving marriage doesn't require pain-free or struggle-free lives. Hope starts as we see that we have something to offer that our spouse appreciates. Hope starts as our needs are touched by our mate. Hope starts as we see a road we can walk together. Seeing the depth of commitment and care within the relationship provides the foundation for trust.

Trust is the willingness to be vulnerable, to communicate one's true feelings and thoughts, and to trust the other person with who we really are. The very nature of a healthy marriage is not two individuals separately living side by side but two people merging their lives together. This means shoring up each other's weaknesses and drawing on each other's strengths.

Les and Andrea say it took another Marriage Encounter weekend to dispel all the garbage between them, to let down all the barriers and "really be us."

"It was a relief to get stuff out in the open and to dispose of the crud between us," says Les. "Once we got it all out, we also realized that with God's help all of our big problems were actually not so big and could be overcome."

After that their communication began to improve. "The first thing was to discuss the children without fighting," Andrea says. "We started to work and plan together. I had to learn to compromise. I still disagree with Les about discipline sometimes. I feel he is harsher than I am. Yet, I began to listen, to hear what Les was saying—that he really did care for me and the children."

For Les, learning to express himself involved more than verbal communication. "It has been helpful for me to be around people who have good marriages. I realized I can let people know that Andrea and I are in love. People in Marriage Encounter show affection by hugging, and it feels good to me now, even with people I don't know very well. Showing affection helped us pull barriers down. It helped me open up and verbalize my disappointments and my hopes."

Expressing affection also helped Les do away with his stereotype of the "macho man." "It took me awhile to accept hugging since I always thought that 'real men' don't do those things. But 'real men' don't care what others think; they are just themselves. Being such a macho man was causing me to miss a lot. I can own my feelings better now than before."

Andrea, too, was inspired by being around couples who had had rough times but came through them. "I was surprised to see what a good marriage is. I wanted it for us. I went after it.

These other couples were stronger because they faced their problems and dealt with them. I, too, wanted to succeed and not have another divorce. I felt personal responsibility for my marriage to Les. I had to accept responsibility for my previous mistakes."

Les agrees. "It was good to see what kind of marriage we could have if we made the effort to really communicate with each other. We finally realized we had to commit ourselves to make our marriage work; it's really a decision on our part to love each other."

"I still get flowers more from other people—my friends or the kids—than my husband," Andrea says slyly, then hastens to add, "but I don't think anymore that we're going to get a divorce just because we occasionally argue over something."

Both Les and Andrea say that since going on the Marriage Encounter weekend, things have only gotten better. But it doesn't mean there haven't been problems; there have. "I guess the important thing is that now we have the knowledge and tools to take care of them quicker before we have time to put walls up between us," says Les. "I don't have to bury my feelings anymore and then wait for them to erupt in the next blowup like I did before."

What are some of the communication tools that Les and Andrea have learned to use?

"Well, for me," Les says, rubbing his beard thoughtfully, "really listening to what Andrea has to say is the first thing, trying to feel what she is feeling. Second, I've had to learn that feelings themselves are neither right nor wrong. They're just feelings. Andrea has her feelings; I have my feelings. We share what we're feeling in order to understand where we're coming from. *Then* we can go on from there and deal with the problem."

Andrea nods. "I had to hear what Les was saying instead of just thinking about what I wanted to say next. That's hard! I also learned to be careful about what I said because once it was said I couldn't take it back. Unfortunately, we still say things that are hurtful. That's why forgiveness is important. I learned to forgive Les for the things I felt he had done to me."

The Baxters also agreed to abide by rules for arguing: focus on the issue, don't bring up the past, don't blame the other person for what you're feeling, give each person a chance to really be heard. "We're still learning how to discuss constructively instead of nit-picking," Andrea admits. "But being listened to makes a big difference."

Knowing that your partner and you are both working at communication gives an air of exploration and learning to the task of building communication. Like a loving parent running along a child's first bike ride without training wheels, we need to encourage, be patient, and be joyous at victory with each other.

Building good communication skills means gearing down. Some conversations need to begin, "I'm not sure how to say this," or, "I'm still struggling with what I'm feeling, but I want to try and explore this with you." As each couple works through life, they develop recipes for success. These recipes include ways to build closeness, *make decisions, solve conflicts, and encourage each other. Each of these recipes include guidelines such as a commitment to honest, non-blaming statements, a willingness to listen and discuss a matter until both people feel totally understood, and a willingness to forgive and seek forgiveness.*

It's important to note that when we feel fully understood and when there is freedom from guilt and resentment, it is often possible to tolerate a few disagreements in a relationship—compromises don't feel like defeats. Over time each healthy couple develops their own style. However, within that style are common fundamentals that can be studied, learned, and incorporated into their life together.

For Andrea, dealing with the past has been an ongoing challenge. "But first," she says, "I quit allowing my daughter to use my past against me. I still feel guilt about it, but I handle it better. Laura tried to do a number on us soon after we had gone to Marriage Encounter, and I stood up to her. She didn't try it again! That was a breakthrough. I felt a lot of relief."

By sharing her feelings of guilt and fear from the past with Les, the walls started coming down. "Les was calm about the relationship with our teenage daughter, and he helped me listen to her. It's funny," says Andrea, smiling wryly, "if the kids have a problem, they tend to go to Les. They know he will discuss it fairly.

"I remember one time, Les had a bad day and was really short-tempered when he came home. I climbed all over him for it. I still tend to get jumpy when someone gets mad because of the fears it brings out. Well, Laura lectured me that Les had a right to a bad mood if he had a bad day, just like I did. Guess I was told, but good!" she says, laughing.

The Baxters have been working to strengthen other areas of their relationship as well. Andrea sometimes calls her husband at work and makes plans for a date. They fix a special meal or go to the movies. They always leave for work with a kiss. They also got involved in the church, helping to sponsor other people who were becoming members.

Andrea says she still tends to clam up

and go read a book rather than argue. "But we're working on that and on other things. I spend too much money, and he has to lecture me about—"

"And I wake up in the morning coughing, and she lectures me that I smoke too much," Les interrupts. "We still have problems—but at least we talk out our problems."

Les and Andrea had to face more serious problems a few years ago when Laura, now twenty-three, became involved in a destructive pattern of drug abuse (alcohol and cocaine). Andrea was devastated to learn that Laura had been sexually abused by Andrea's second husband—a fact that finally came out in Laura's deep anger that Andrea did not protect her as a mother should. Laura had been afraid to tell because he had threatened to kill her brother and mom if she did.

"The last two years have been a nightmare of frustration and despair," Andrea says. "I see that the chemical dependence is a symptom of much deeper problems. But I wonder when she will realize that we were all victims, and that eventually she has to forgive herself—just as I do to prevent being emotionally crippled all our lives."

Andrea attends support groups for co-dependents, and she has been learning just how destructive the patterns can be that are handed down from generation to generation. "My parents weren't alcoholics," she says, "but my father was the child of an alcoholic, and my mother was abused. The question I am dealing with is: In what generation do we break this destructive pattern?"

But Andrea feels that there is hope in healing and forgiveness. Laura is seeking counseling and appears to be trying to stay off chemicals. And where does Les figure in all this? "He is the commonsense factor in our story," Andrea says. "He is the strength and love that have kept me from totally disintegrating in this recent difficulty. What we learned about communication in our marriage has enabled us to stand together in this rough period of our lives."

In many ways the problems the Baxters face now with their daughter are much more serious than the problems they had when they first got married. "But learning to communicate was the key," Andrea says. "Without it there'd be no recovery of hope. We grew through our struggles and became a different couple. I was no longer the old Andrea; I was a new Andrea with hope."

CHAPTER FOUR

Talking That Works

"And what attracted you to each other?"
I asked the couple in marital despair.
Time after time in counseling, I ask this
question, and time after time the response comes: "Oh, she was such a good
listener." "He was so interesting and was
always supportive." "He was easy to talk
to. We used to talk every day, sometimes
for hours. We could talk about anything."

So what has happened when you
can't talk anymore?

Many romances begin with a large
quantity of intense communication.
This is because the early interactions are
usually filled with a strong motivation
to please each other. Also, there is a
high tolerance for irritations and a

strong drive that catapults the relationship to the top of our time and energy
priorities. Couples "falling in love" talk
a lot, spend much time together, and
think a lot about the relationship.

My wife and I both enjoy picnics,
parties, and pizza. We did at sixteen,
and we do today, and I'm glad that we
do. But we are both much more complicated than a simple set of likes and dis-
likes, and our marriage wouldn't make
it if it were based on a few things we
have in common. The world we live in
throws new dilemmas at us daily.

What do I think? What does she feel?
What pressures are we under? How will
we react? Every day of life together
brings a mixture of predictable and unpredictable reactions and responses,
and the communication required to
deal with these takes time. In a world
with fast food, worldwide satellite
hookups, and fax machines, the subtle-
ties of a couple's communication cannot
be conducted during TV commercials,
while pausing at a stoplight, or while
standing in line at the movies. Communication must take priority in a planned

way with both spouses deciding to take the time. In order to reestablish positive patterns, some couples have found it useful to set weekly or twice-weekly appointments when they set aside time to do nothing but talk and work out problems.

Take the Time to Listen

Good communication in marriage means we are staying current with the status of our own life and with each other. When communication breaks down, the exchange of love breaks down. Love is active. Love works together and requires a specific back-and-forth exchange.

Imagine that you are being examined by your doctor. The first question is, Where does it hurt? This question sets up the first step in communication. You must evaluate yourself and identify what is going on. Identifying emotions is harder than pin-pointing an upset stomach or a broken leg, but it can be done.

One of the most common communication pitfalls is the tendency to tell the other person what he should do without identifying where it hurts. No doctor wants to start a treatment without a diagnosis. No couple solves a problem without first bringing it into awareness.

Next, clear statements need to be shared. Putting your finger on the spot helps the exam move faster than saying, "I don't know," or "Somewhere around here." Communication filled with "I'm feeling glad that . . ." or "I'm scared because . . ." helps focus the exchange. Further questions, discussion, and clarification can then take place. Sometimes, listening and understanding are all that is needed.

Decisions need to be made; problems must be solved. But to do this effectively, hearing the pain or pleasure is vital. When we are connecting, we experience our spouse as aware, supportive, and loving. When we are not connecting, distance, defensiveness, and disappointment set in.

Focus the Purpose of Your Communication
Communication goes much better when we agree on the purpose. Some of the main purposes are:

- *The desire to share.* Don't forget that an experience or thought that is shared provides a feeling of partnership.
- *The desire to change.* When discomfort is communicated, there is an opportunity to brainstorm and problem solve together.
- *The desire to receive.* We are encouraged and built up when someone pays us the compliment of wanting to learn from us.
- *The desire to care.* We draw together when we reach out to help.
- *The desire to be cared for.* We draw closer together when we trust enough to seek help.

Never Assume What Hasn't Been Said

Whenever you are surprised by your spouse's response, *stop!* Ask your partner what he or she *thought* you were saying.

Whenever you are frustrated and don't think your spouse is understanding, *stop!* Examine yourself, and begin with a clear, noncritical statement of what you are feeling.

Sometimes the clearest statement we can make is, "Something's bothering me." If this is where you are, take responsibility for gaining that much clarity. It's worth it. Each person must define his or her own feelings. Marriage communication runs terrible risks when generalizations are used. Saying things like, "Oh, you know what I mean," or "I know how you feel," may not be helpful; the other person might *not* understand. Too often love gets confused with mind reading. Be clear. Share together, pray, meditate, write—do whatever it takes to focus your thoughts and feelings.

Whenever you sense you are not getting anywhere, *stop!* Ask your spouse what he or she thinks is going on inside him or her and what is going on inside you.

Risk Openness and Honesty

Worrying about what would happen "if he [or she] ever found out" is to live under a powerful and terrible cloud of fear. Fear is like a wound left uncleaned; it infects and injects poison throughout our lives until confronted and confessed.

Consider the husband who is feeling lonely, tired, and unappreciated. Rather than share these thoughts directly—for fear they will not be responded to well or because he is unaware of them in the first place—suppose he says, "Honey, how about making my favorite meal for supper tonight?"

Because the husband has not exposed his feelings, his wife can only respond to what he said. She might be feeling overworked or overwhelmed herself, in which case she might wonder how he dares to make extra demands on her. But rather than reveal her true feelings, she might put out her own little test of whether he cares: "Let's go out to eat!"

Thinking that she doesn't care about him enough to do something nice, the sparks could fly as he snaps, "You know we don't have the money!"

"We would if you didn't waste it!"

"All I asked for was one simple little meal, and you can't even do that."

"What have you done for me?"

And on and on it can go until we have

two lonely people, far from their basic feelings, attacking and hurting each other when they had no intention of doing harm. This is one way failure to be open and honest kills love.

Don't Put Down the Other's Feelings

Unlike the early days of dating, when you only put your best foot forward, marriage provides a chance to be known by another person almost as well as you know yourself. Being loved by one who truly knows you is one of the great gifts of marriage, but it is risky because you could be rejected.

Therefore, if we are going to be open and honest with each other, we must also be careful with each other's feelings. Lines such as, "You shouldn't feel that way," or, "How can you say such a thing?" shut off communication. These messages and others like them teach us to keep quiet, screen our thoughts, and say only the "right things." Unfortunately, if we try to tell our feelings how we want them to be, we lose. Day after day our feelings crank out all types of reactions to the world around us. Why we feel or think the way we do isn't always easy to understand and is even harder to stop.

Don't Try to Fix What Ain't Broken

Many conflicts begin when one spouse *does* share a feeling in an honest and open way and the other person thinks it is a request for change. "I wish we had more money" could be a simple statement of a desire. If so, the spouse might respond, "So do I," or "I'm content with our income, why is it bothering you?" But, if it's heard as a need for change— or worse yet, an accusation of inadequacy—a defensive response might be given: "I do the best I can with what we've got" or "I'm working as hard as I can" or "Why are you blaming me? Why don't you get a job yourself?"

Whenever an innocent conversation quickly turns into fighting, *stop!* Ask each other what is the purpose—the intent—of this conversation. Did the person really intend to accuse the other person? Did he or she mean to introduce a decision about changing their life-style? Or was it just a *wish* being expressed? Whether we are in a simple sharing mode or want to initiate an evaluation and decision-making conversation needs to be jointly agreed upon.

Clear Away the Little Annoyances

Feelings are a part of who we are. They need to be shared. They need to be heard. They may or may not be accommodated, but working through feelings as a couple can shift the marriage from anger and blame to a process of healing and growth.

Consider this silly but helpful example. Early in the couple's married life, the wife fixes a lovely supper that includes lima beans. Now, the young husband doesn't like lima beans. Does he:

1. Try not to eat them and hope she doesn't notice?
2. Eat them, smile, and say they are great?
3. Not eat them, not say anything, but hope she does notice?
4. Say he doesn't like them and discuss what to do?

If he decides to talk about it, he should first thank his wife for the nice supper. Then he might try to find out whether she cooked the lima beans because *she* likes them or because she thought *he* liked them. Next, he might communicate his preferences and try to reach some agreement that satisfies both. If this communication doesn't take place, years of bitterness may build as the husband continues to eat something he doesn't like and is angry at his wife for continuing to fix it. A silly story? Yes—but lots of marital fights follow this pattern.

If we are not bothered by something or the annoyance was temporary and largely passed . . . OK. No mention needs to be made. As maturity grows, so does tolerance. But if we can't let it go— small as it might be—attention needs to be given to it. There is nothing wrong with talking about small annoyances. Do it clearly, quickly, and move on. The Bible recommends not going to bed angry. That wisdom is still the best prescription for marital communication today.

Don't Run from Differences

One of the reasons for keeping the little matters cleared up is that we all face big areas of disagreement or disappointment with each other from time to time. They can be handled much more successfully if the table is clear of the little hurts.

So what should be done with true differences of opinion? Differences do add to the work of getting along with each other, but they don't need to stop the flow of love. Couples often can agree on the broad strokes of how they want things to be: happy lives, healthy kids, getting along with each other. But how to get there? That's the rub.

However, navigating our differences can be managed with greater ease under the following conditions:

- the belief that two heads are really better than one
- a commitment to respect each other while working together
- the resolve to stay in the struggle until a mutual agreement is reached

Following these guidelines creates the best chances for resolving genuine differences.

Some couples are helped by discussing genuine differences with a wise and mutually trusted friend. Sometimes the deliberate effort of just sitting down and talking out the pros and cons of a matter tips the balance to finding a new alternative or reaching a *workable* compromise. Sometimes the third party can help them hear each other better.

Be Quick to Make Peace

Some of our hardest conversations involve discussions of our weaknesses, insecurities, wrong thinking, and wrong doing. Our whole nature resists it. We try to shift the focus, make excuses, blame someone or something else. But honesty opens the door to understanding, healing, forgiveness, and hope.

For the couples in this book to be reconciled, they had to exercise great courage in starting to talk again. Hearing about the ways you have hurt your spouse—both unintentionally and in-

tentionally—is tough. Sharing disappointments and limitations is scary.

Communication can also require
great faith. Stating a difference or feeling
of hurt to your spouse is risky. Hearing
the neediness and humanness of your
spouse can be overwhelming. Many
deeply broken couples need a professional counselor to guide the process.
But in time, each of the couples in this
book learned how to find support and
direction for relating in new and healing
ways.

Farewell

The true stories you have read in this
book are gifts of love. Love made them
possible. Love caused them to be told so
that *you* can learn to talk together again.

The Recovery of Hope movement is a
network of couples who care about
marriages. They care about hurting
spouses because they've each been one.
Let their stories be a gift of hope, an act
of love, and a sacred trust that God's
reconciling power will be available to
you each day.

CHAPTER FIVE

What Is Recovery of Hope?

Recovery of Hope is a program for couples who are experiencing disillusionment in their marriages. Some may be contemplating divorce. The program recognizes that problems and disillusionment are normal in a marriage. However, many couples give up because they do not know what else to do.

Couples register for a three-hour session where a team of three alumni couples share their own experiences of disillusionment and the events and insights that created a spark of hope for them to attempt reconciliation. The new couples then consider their situation and how they are feeling about it. To aid in reaching a decision, a counselor will meet with the couple to help them tailor a plan to meet their needs. The reconciliation plan may include such things as counseling, meeting with a support group, programs for help in planning finances, parenting, and/or any other service that would be helpful.

ROH is based on sound psychological principles and basic spiritual values along with acceptance and support from volunteers and professionals. It provides a couple with time to review their marriage and make a decision about their future. While ROH is forthright in being "pro-marriage," it is most of all pro-health. Participants' decisions are honored and respected.

If you are struggling in your marriage or feel like giving up, you may wish to contact the Recovery of Hope Network. To find the program nearest you, call 1-800-327-2590 in the U.S. and Canada.

Other Living Books Best-sellers

101 FUN BIBLE CROSSWORDS. Young and old alike will discover hours of brain-teasing, mind-stretching, vocabulary-building fun in this puzzle-packed collection. All puzzle themes relate to Bible facts, characters, and terms. 07-0976-4

400 CREATIVE WAYS TO SAY I LOVE YOU by Alice Chapin. Perhaps the flame of love has almost died in your marriage, or you have a good marriage that just needs a little spark. Here is a book of creative, practical ideas for the woman who wants to show the man in her life that she cares. 07-0919-5

ANSWERS by Josh McDowell and Don Stewart. In a question-and-answer format, the authors tackle sixty-five of the most-asked questions about the Bible, God, Jesus Christ, miracles, other religions, and creation. 07-0021-X

BUILDING YOUR SELF-IMAGE by Josh McDowell and Don Stewart. Here are practical answers to help you overcome your fears, anxieties, and lack of self-confidence. Learn how God's higher image of who you are can take root in your heart and mind. 07-1395-8

THE CHILD WITHIN by Mari Hanes. The author shares insights she gained from God's Word during her own pregnancy. She identifies areas of stress, offers concrete data about the birth process, and points to God's sure promises that he will gently lead those that are with young. 07-0219-0

COME BEFORE WINTER AND SHARE MY HOPE by Charles R. Swindoll. A collection of brief vignettes offering hope and the assurance that adversity and despair are temporary setbacks we can overcome! 07-0477-0

DR. DOBSON ANSWERS YOUR QUESTIONS by Dr. James Dobson. In this convenient reference book, re-nowned author Dr. James Dobson addresses heartfelt concerns on many topics, including questions on marital relationships, infant care, child discipline, home management, and others. 07-0580-7

DR. DOBSON ANSWERS YOUR QUESTIONS: RAISING CHILDREN by Dr. James Dobson. A renowned authority on child-rearing offers his expertise on the spiritual training of children, sex education, discipline, coping with adolescence, and more. 07-1104-1

Other Living Books Best-sellers

FOR MEN ONLY edited by J. Allan Petersen. This book deals with topics of concern to every man: the business world, marriage, fathering, spiritual goals, and problems of living as a Christian in a secular world. 07-0892-X

FOR WOMEN ONLY by Evelyn and J. Allan Petersen. A balanced, entertaining, diversified treatment of all the aspects of womanhood. 07-0897-0

GIVERS, TAKERS, AND OTHER KINDS OF LOVERS by Josh McDowell and Paul Lewis. Bypassing generalities about love and sex, this book answers the basics: Whatever happened to sexual freedom? Do men respond differently than women? Here are straight answers about God's plan for love and sexuality. 07-1031-2

HINDS' FEET ON HIGH PLACES by Hannah Hurnard. A classic allegory of a journey toward faith that has sold more than a million copies! 07-1429-6

JOHN, SON OF THUNDER by Ellen Gunderson Traylor. In this saga of adventure, romance, and discovery, travel with John—the disciple whom Jesus loved—down desert paths, through the courts of the Holy City, and to the foot of the cross as he leaves his luxury as a privileged son of Israel for the bitter hardship of his exile on Patmos. 07-1903-4

LET ME BE A WOMAN by Elisabeth Elliot. This best-selling author combines her observations and experiences in a number of essays on male-female relationships. 07-2162-4

LIFE IS TREMENDOUS! by Charlie "Tremendous" Jones. Believing that enthusiasm makes the difference, Jones shows how anyone can be happy, involved, relevant, productive, healthy, and secure in the midst of a high-pressure, commercialized society. 07-2184-5

LORD, COULD YOU HURRY A LITTLE? by Ruth Harms Calkin. These prayer-poems from the heart of a godly woman trace the inner workings of the heart, following the rhythms of the day and seasons of the year with expectation and love. 07-3816-0

LORD, I KEEP RUNNING BACK TO YOU by Ruth Harms Calkin. In prayer-poems tinged with wonder, joy, humanness, and questioning, the author speaks for all of us who are groping and learning together what it means to be God's child. 07-3819-5

Other Living Books Best-sellers

MORE THAN A CARPENTER by Josh McDowell. A hard-hitting book for people who are skeptical about Jesus' deity, his resurrection, and his claim on their lives. 07-4552-3

MOUNTAINS OF SPICES by Hannah Hurnard. Here is an allegory comparing the nine spices mentioned in the Song of Solomon to the nine fruits of the Spirit. A story of the glory of surrender by the author of *Hinds' Feet on High Places*. 07-4611-2

OUT OF THE STORM by Grace Livingston Hill. Gail finds herself afloat on an angry sea, desperately trying to keep an unconscious man from slipping away from her. 07-4778-X

THE RANSOM by Grace Livingston Hill. Following her step-mother's death, Christobel and her family must learn to trust and love each other as they begin a new life. Then her impetuous brother Randall is kidnapped—and Christobel must find a way to free him before it is too late. 07-5143-4

THE SEARCH FOR THE TWELVE APOSTLES by William Steuart McBirnie. Through travel, Bible study, and research, McBirnie has uncovered the history of Christ's apostles and their evangelical activities. The dedication and zeal of these men will inspire the faith of every reader. 07-5839-0

THE SECRET OF LOVING by Josh McDowell. McDowell explores the values and qualities that will help both the single and married reader to be the right person for someone else. He offers a fresh perspective for evaluating and improving the reader's love life. 07-5845-5

THE STORY FROM THE BOOK. From Adam to Armageddon, this book captures the full sweep of the Bible's content in abridged, chronological form. Based on *The Book*, the best-selling, popular edition of *The Living Bible*. 07-6677-6

THE STRONG-WILLED CHILD by Dr. James Dobson. With practical solutions and humorous anecdotes, Dobson shows how to discipline an assertive child without breaking his spirit. Parents will learn to overcome feelings of defeat or frustration by setting boundaries and taking action. 07-5924-9

SUCCESS! THE GLENN BLAND METHOD by Glenn Bland. The author shows how to set goals and make plans that really work. His ingredients of success include spiritual, financial, educational, and recreational balances. 07-6689-X

Other Living Books Best-sellers

One morning as Bob was about ready to go off to work, Rhonda handed him a note:

I'm tired: tired of hearing your excuses for not doing things around the house, tired of you being late, tired of you making us late because of your long hours. I'm tired of having to do all the child-care and housework. We really need to take time to talk and work out some things!

"What's this?" Bob asked.

"A note. Just read it!" snapped Rhonda.

"I did. But why a note? Can't you just talk to me?"

When Bob and Rhonda got married, they were happy and looked forward to many wonderful years together. But then things began to change, and the level of tension in the house went up. Maybe it was pressures of raising the kids . . . differing expectations . . . the long hours of overtime. Whatever the causes, it was clear that Bob and Rhonda's marriage was in trouble.

As you read the true stories in this book, you'll get to know couples who had despaired to the point of divorce of ever being able to talk constructively and lovingly again. And you'll also learn how they learned new ways to communicate and recovered hope for their relationship.